AMERICAN LIVES   Series Editor: Tobias Wolff

Turning Bones

Lee Martin

UNIVERSITY OF NEBRASKA PRESS : LINCOLN & LONDON

Acknowledgments for the
use of previously published
material appear on page 195.

Typeset in Adobe Minion.
Book design: R. Eckersley

Library of Congress Cataloging-in-Publication-Data
Turning bones / Lee Martin.
p. cm. – (American lives)
ISBN 0-8032-3231-4 (cloth: alkaline paper)
1. Farmers – Fiction. 2. Farm life – Fiction. 3. Illinois –
Fiction. 4. Domestic fiction, American. 5. Historical
fiction, American. 6. Martin, Lee, 1955 – Family.
7. Martin, Lee, 1955 – Childhood and youth. 8. Martin,
Lee – Homes and haunts – Illinois. I. Title. II. Series.
PS3563.A724927T87 2003 813'.54–dc21 2003007966

For Deb

Contents

Acknowledgments

Turning Bones is a work of fact and fiction, and I could have never accomplished the first if not for the kind assistance of a number of people, some of them generous strangers, and some of them distant relatives whom I never would have known had I not become curious about my ancestors. Many thanks to Kim Coles, Pat DeArman Fite, Donna Dye Geddings, Nancy Hesler, Diane Keeton, and Kitty Lee Twarog for their willingness to share family history with me. My gratitude, also, to the kind people of Nicholas County, Kentucky; Brown County, Ohio; and Lawrence County and Richland County, Illinois. Finally, a big hug for my wife, Deb, for tolerating the many trips to libraries and courthouses and cemeteries. There's no one else I'd rather have with me on the journey.

I'm indebted to my early readers – Lee K. Abbott, David Citino, Michelle Herman, Joe Mackall, Jim Phelan, Ladette Randolph, and Bill Roorbach – and to the editors at the journals who were kind enough to publish portions of this book: Donna Baer Stein, Jerome Lowenstein, and Danielle Ofri at the *Bellevue Literary Review*; Dinty Moore at *Brevity*; Michael Steinberg and David Cooper at *Fourth Genre;* John Dufresne at Gulf Stream; Lex Williford at *Natural Bridge*; and Hilda Raz at *Prairie Schooner.*

Thanks, too, to the University of North Texas, the Texas Commission on the Arts, and the National Endowment for the Arts for supporting the beginning of this work, and to The Ohio State University for its favor as the book came to its end.

Nicholas Gaunce
m: Prudence

Martin family tree

George Gaunce
m: Sarah Martin
[her sibling: James Martin]

James Martin

George Ridgley
m: Mary Strouse

John A. Martin 1810-1898
m1: Elizabeth Gaunce 1810-1867
m2: Eliza French Phillips 1846-1918
[his siblings:
Sarah ("Hethy") m: Reuben Fite,
Malinda m: Joseph Fite]

Clarissa Ridgley 1827-1916
m1: Jonathan Inyart 1827-1852
m2: William Bell

John Delbert Martin
[his siblings: Cora, Anora, Lula]

James Henry ("Henry") Martin
1843-1920
m: Mary Ann Inyart 1849-1919
[his siblings by the marriage of John A. Martin
and Elizabeth Gaunce:
William, Sarah ("Sally") m: Alfred Ridgley,
Nancy A., George, Prudence Louisa ("Lou"),
Jackson m: Matilda Fite, Robert m: Ursula Fite]
[her siblings: William, Marion, Amy, John,
Mary Ann ("Annie")]

George William ("Will") Martin 1875-1901
[his sibling:
Charles ("Charlie") Martin m: Clara Hill — Omer]
m1: Phoebe Ellen ("Ella") Preston
m2: Stella Ethel Inyart 1883-1965

Glen
Mae

Roy Martin 1913-1982
m: Beulah Read 1910-1988
[his siblings: Leona Ferne,
Florence Edna,
Lola Mildred, William Owen]

Lee Martin b. 1955
m: Debra Goss b. 1957

1
Decoration Day

Long ago, each year at the end of May, I helped my mother pick peonies and irises and then arrange them into bouquets. The peonies were my favorite. I remember their sweet scent and the ruffles of their blooms, some of them as broad as my mother's hand. They grew on lush green bushes beneath the maple trees that separated our side yard from our vegetable garden. The irises let down their brilliant beards from the stalks that came up each spring along the wire fence that enclosed our front yard.

While my mother snipped the irises – purple and yellow – and the peonies – crimson and white – it was my job to wrap coffee cans with foil paper. It was Decoration Day, and we were going to the cemeteries to put flowers on the family graves, the generations of Martins who had preceded my father and me, who had come from Kentucky by way of Ohio and settled in Lukin Township in southeastern Illinois.

I knew nothing of death then. I was a child, and I lived on a farm where I had eighty acres of woodland and pasture and prairie to explore. It was the beginning of summer. The days were warm, and each evening it was longer and longer before darkness came. Our farm was on the county line, a gravel road that separated our county, Lawrence, from the next county, Richland. The official surveyor's description announced that we owned the south half of the northwest quarter of section eighteen, township two north, range thirteen west of the second prime meridian. Our house sat a half-mile off the road at the end of a lane lined with hickory trees and oaks, with sassafras and milkweed. Tiger lilies and black-eyed Susans grew wild in the fence rows, as did blackberries and honeysuckle and multiflora rose.

On summer days I ran barefoot over the grass, arms outstretched to catch the winged seedlings that came twirling down from our maple trees. I walked deep into our woods and listened to the squirrels chattering and the woodpeckers drilling. I waded through the shallow water of creek beds to see the tracks that raccoons and coyotes had left. When I came out into open prairie, I lay down in pockets of grass where deer had slept and stared up at the wide, blue sky.

In my child's mind I had a sovereign claim to those eighty acres. At dusk I stood outside and shouted my name for the sheer joy of hearing it echo back to me. *Lee, Lee, Lee.* The air itself seemed to announce my dominion. I had no thought that there had been other boys before me who had done the same thing. When darkness finally fell and the fireflies came out, I caught them in my hand and dropped them into a Mason jar. I can still recall the sensation of their wings pulsing against my palm, that tickle that told me I had caught them, that they were mine now to do with what I chose.

When I went with my parents to the cemeteries, I knew little about the ancestors whose graves we adorned with our bouquets. I had known my grandmother, Stella, but never my grandfather, Will, who had died fourteen years before I was born. The others – James Henry, Mary Ann, John, Owen, Lola – were only sounds to me, a collection of consonants and vowels. They meant nothing. I knew more intimately the irises and the peonies and how my mother weighted the coffee cans with gravel scooped from our lane. I knew the sparkle of the foil paper and the smell of freshly cut grass at the cemeteries.

On one of our visits, I started to run – it seems that I was always running, then – and my mother caught me by my arm. "Don't run across the graves," she said.

"Why?" I asked her.

Now I think of peonies in winter, when they die back and the little red buds on their crowns – their "eyes" – stare up through the frozen ground and wait for spring.

My mother put a finger to her lips. "Shh," she said in a whisper I had to lean close to hear. "People are sleeping here," she told me. "Don't wake them."

2
Kentucky

Somewhere on the Atlantic Ocean, in 1723, a child was born to a family named Martin, and they called him John. Only three days had passed since they had sailed from Ireland, their course set for America. I like to think of this child, who would never know the land of his father, taking breath and opening his eyes there on the wide expanse of ocean. His mother and father must have seen him as a promise of prosperity: a new babe, a new land, life beginning.

There would have been fevers and dysentery, storms and sea sickness, ocean swells and blistering heat. John's mother would have held him to her breast through all of it, feeling his strong pull at her nipple, the kneading of his tiny hands. "A strong one thee art," she might have murmured, believing in his determined feeding, in the trade wind pushing them west, the bow cleaving the water until eventually (a month or two or three might have passed) the fresh scent of forests drifted to her – the smell of cedar and pine – and one day someone called out, "Land! Praise the Lord! Land!"

I like to imagine that this John Martin is my ancestor, although I have no proof that I descended from his blood. My research into my family line has uncovered a gaggle of Johns and Jameses, and it's been difficult to untangle them and to say with certainty which is my direct ancestor. I do know, however, that my great-great-grandmother, Elizabeth Gaunce, descended from a family who came to America from the Rhineland of southwestern Germany, an area known as Palatinate. There, in 1708, the winter was so severe that many Palatine Germans, who had suffered the slaughter of war and the ruin of their farms, fled. More than twelve thousand sought refuge in England and from there sailed to America, most of them making their way to Pennsylvania.

It is there that I first discover families by the name of Gaunce and Martin living near one another. The 1790 census for Washington

County lists in Cecil Township a Benjamin, George, and Nicholas Gaunce, as well as a James Martin. A land plat shows the farm of Nicholas Gaunce bordering that of James Martin. The two names appear again on the 1810 census of Nicholas County, Kentucky. There, in 1797, when Nicholas County has yet to be formed from parts of Bourbon and Mason Counties, Nicholas's son, George, marries for the second time, his first wife having died only two months earlier. His second wife is Sarah Martin; I can only speculate that she is the sister of James Martin, who has migrated to Kentucky along with the Gaunces. George and Sarah will give birth to ten children; the sixth will be my great-great-grandmother, Elizabeth, born in July of 1810, five months after my great-great-grandfather, John A. Martin, has come into the world.

The Martins and Gaunces own land along the Johnston Fork of the Licking River near a community known as Saltwell. Their farms are up in the hills, their log homes built deep in the hollows; often the only visible sign of them is the smoke rising from a fireplace chimney. How excited little John and Elizabeth must be when from time to time one of the families climbs the hills, finds the trails along the ridges, and makes its way to the other's home. There are quilting bees, corn huskings, taffy pulls. I imagine Elizabeth with blond hair in pigtails, John with the long arms and narrow shoulders I've inherited from my grandfather. And the jug ears, too big for a boy his age, sticking out too far from his head. By the time he's twelve, he's started to feel self-conscious of his gangly body. And despite the fact that Elizabeth is his own cousin – his father's sister's daughter – he's started to notice how her hair feels when sometimes the end of a pigtail tickles his arm.

One day all of the children are gathered around a fire outside the Gaunces', where the grownups are boiling down cane juice from sorghum. Soon the boys and girls will get to scrape the candied molasses from the sides of the tin box, blow the sweet gobs cool, and eat them. But first Elizabeth's sister, Prudence, decides to stir up trouble. She's jealous because it's become clear that John is sweet on Elizabeth and not on her.

"You look like an old mule," Prudence says to John, and soon the two youngest Gaunce boys, Zedekiah and Moses, are braying in John's face. "Hee-haw! Hee-haw!"

And Elizabeth grabs John's hand, and together they run into the woods. Prudence and Zed and Moses don't follow, because after all there's all that molasses, the promise of its sweet taste enough to keep them put.

Deep in the woods, where the red oak and poplar and dogwood have yet to drop their leaves, John holds Elizabeth's hand and feels her heart racing in a vein in her palm. All his life he will remember this pulsing, how he held her hand until her heartbeat slowed, there in the shade, in the cool dark, the sounds of Zed's and Moses's braying fading from his ears. He'll remember how, finally, he and Elizabeth turned and walked back to the others, no words passing between them, only a silent acknowledgment that they were, from that day on, bound together as one.

When I was a boy, a family named Jent lived on the next farm north. There were three brothers – David, Donnie, and Dan, in descending order – and a sister my age named Katrina. I was an only child of older parents – my mother was forty-five when I was born; my father, forty-two – so all of my cousins were young adults by the time I came along. Katrina was the first girl to ever come into my life, and she fascinated me. Sometimes she and Dan walked across our fields, and we spent the afternoon at play. On occasion I did the same, although I didn't like making this trip. There were barbed-wire fences to climb over or crawl through, and I was always afraid I would snag myself on one of the sharp barbs. I preferred to let Katrina come for me and then accompany me through the fields, holding the barbed wire apart so I could make my way safely to the other side.

I was a timid child, not meant for the rough ways of farm life. There was so much that frightened me: the barbed wire, the water moccasins at the Jents' pond, the bulls in their pasture, the bees that hovered over the clover blossoms. Everything seemed dangerous. I was particularly afraid of the Jents' dog, a terrier that growled at me and nipped at my ankles. Whenever I came to visit, Katrina locked the dog in the shed, and no matter how much Dan protested, she insisted that the dog stay there so I wouldn't be afraid.

In my own home my father whipped me at the least provocation. He used his belt, and sometimes a yardstick or a persimmon switch. When I was barely a year old, he had lost both his hands when a corn picker mangled them beyond saving. He wore prosthetic hooks, their steel as cold and as hard as the regret that shadowed his life. There was so much to disappoint him. He had lost his hands because of his own carelessness; he had tried to clear the picker's shucking box without first shutting down the tractor's power takeoff, the device that sent the shucking box's rollers spinning, the rollers that pulled in his hands. Only a year before, I had come into his life abruptly, a surprise. My parents hadn't planned on having children, and when they did, I turned out to be the sort of son I'm sure my father wouldn't have chosen. I was afraid of the dark, of the sparrows that sometimes got into our house, of the snakes that slithered through our yard. My father's response to my fainthearted nature was one of anger. Sometimes when he whipped me, I tried to run away, and he chased me about our farm yard, the air filling with our shouts.

"Goodness," my mother said once. "The Jents will think there's murder going on."

It shamed me to think that Katrina might be outside listening to the ugly shouts and screams and curses coming from our farm. What would she think of me? That I was, as my father often claimed, a heathen? I feared that the next time I saw her she would turn away from me in disgust. But she never did. If she knew my trouble, she never mentioned it.

We were kids, only six years old, and we lived on farms separated by wide expanses of fields. I used to stand outside my house and gaze across those flat fields, hoping to catch some sign of her in her farm yard, which rested atop a hill – a flash of a red jacket, perhaps, the sparkle of the gold barrettes that she wore in her curled black hair – and then I would hope that she might walk across those fields to me. She was the sister I never had, the one I looked for as an adult in every new place I lived. She was a kind and merciful presence at the time of my father's rage, and for that I loved her.

In the summer of 1989 my wife and I left our apartment in Memphis and rented half a duplex in Olney, Illinois, Deb's hometown. We would only stay two months. Come August, we would return to Memphis and get ready for the start of the fall semester at the university where we both taught. We had lived away from southern Illinois for eight years, and now a research grant had given us the chance to return. I looked on our two months as an opportunity to get some writing done and, perhaps more important, to reconnect with the people and the land I had left.

I grew up twelve miles to the east of Olney, in Lawrence County. My first home was the family farm in Lukin Township, and then, after a six-year move to a southern suburb of Chicago, my parents bought a modest frame house on Locust Street in Sumner, a small village off Highway 50 between Olney and Vincennes, Indiana.

My father had leased our ground while we lived up north, but after we moved to Sumner, he again took over the farm. During planting season, he rousted me out of bed shortly after first light.

"Day's wasting," he said. "Let's go."

We drove south on the Sumner-Lancaster blacktop until we reached what was known as the Bethlehem Corner, the gravel road that ran west past the Christian Church. We followed the road to its "T," made the dogleg jog left and then right, and went on to the county line. There, a quarter of a mile to the south, the tin roof of our barn gleamed silver in the sunlight, the red brick chimney of our farmhouse appeared between the branches of the maple tree in the front yard.

To me, as a teenager, our farm was a place of torment. When I would rather have been doing anything else, I spent long, hot days plowing and disking and planting. The sun burned my skin, the dust coated my clothes, the hot exhaust of the tractor flew up into my face. I knew early on that I wasn't made for such work – not that I was incapable; I simply had no interest.

"Are you going to be a farmer like your father?" Deb asked me on our first date.

"Not a chance," I said.

Later she told me that if I had said yes, she wouldn't have given me a second look. "There was no way I was going to be a farmer's wife."

This was in 1975, at the end of a period of inflation. Crop prices were bringing in less income than what farmers paid in production expenses, and the oil shortage took fuel prices to an all-time high, "putting the clamps on the short hairs," as my father said. By 1979 interest rates had risen to 18 percent. President Carter imposed a grain embargo after the Russians invaded Afghanistan. Then the bottom dropped out of land values. Farmland that had been selling for up to fifteen hundred dollars per acre was only worth five hundred dollars. The decline of small family farms had begun. By 1970 their number had shrunk from a peak of 6.8 million in 1935 to fewer than 3 million. My father was twenty-two in 1935, and his vision for himself stretched no further than the eighty acres he would one day inherit from my grandfather. I was fifteen in 1970, nineteen in 1975, and every occupation I had considered – history teacher, minister, basketball coach, journalist – had nothing to do with farming.

But that summer of 1989 no one was forcing me to work that land; it wasn't holding me hostage. I was free to move through it at my own will, relearning its contours, its flora and fauna. I marveled over the flash of white tail feathers as quail performed their bobbing flight patterns, a field of timothy grass undulating in waves, the prickly purple heads of garlic gone to seed along the fence rows of wheat fields.

One day I went to visit my aunt Ferne, my father's sister. My father had died in 1982, my mother in 1988, and my aunt was one of the few relatives left who could tell me anything about my family's history. On this day she told me that the Martins had come to Illinois from Ohio, that my great-grandfather, James Henry, and my great-grandmother, Mary Ann, had lived in a log house on what was now my farm. We sat on the sofa in my aunt's living room, its back lined with family photographs in frames, photos of her grandchildren and great-grandchildren and her sons; the younger of the two, Philip, shared her house and sat across from us in a rocking chair. The drapes were closed, and no lamps were on to light the darkness.

"Grandpa raised tobacco for twists," Aunt Ferne said. "I used to pick worms off the plants. And he had rail fences around all the lots. Grandma made crullers. Oh, I did like those crullers. And beans. I loved the way she cooked beans."

Aunt Ferne showed me an old photo of Henry and Mary Ann toward the ends of their lives. They were sitting in chairs on a wooden walkway that led down from their log house. The first thing I noticed was Henry's long white hair, combed forward over his ears, hiding them, I knew – those Martin ears that were too big and stuck out too far.

"Who was Henry's father?" I asked Aunt Ferne.

"His name was John," she said. "John Martin. He's buried in the Ridgley Cemetery."

"What was his wife's name?"

"Oh, you've got so many questions. His wife? Let me see. I don't think I rightly know."

The Ridgley Cemetery is located in Lukin Township on the old Ridgley family farm, along a gravel road that runs parallel to the Sumner-Lancaster blacktop, three crossroads north of our farm. I found it after I left my aunt's, relying on my vague memories of visiting it with my parents on Decoration Day. My father used to drive the township roads on Sunday afternoons, taking us so deep into the country I swore we'd never find our way home. But he always knew exactly where he was going, took pride, even, in the fact that he knew the landscape so well.

I took a similar satisfaction in being able to find the road that led to the Ridgley Cemetery, recalling, as I drove, the curve and dip and the long hill shaded by the trees that spread their branches over its grade. I remembered the way the hill finally plateaued and how the cemetery was in a clearing off to the right. I pulled off the road, parking in the weeds that grew along the ditch, and saw the long wire gate that opened to the cemetery and the white faces of tombstones filing back to the tree line. On Decoration Day my father always made sure that the gate was closed when we left. It was something a good farmer knew. If you opened a gate, you closed it behind you.

When I opened the gate to the cemetery that day and began to walk among the tombstones, I didn't know that I was taking the responsibility of chasing my family's story. Over the next eleven years I would talk to relatives, interview strangers, post queries on the Internet, study family photographs, and poke around in county courthouses, looking at land plats, deeds, records of births, marriages, and deaths. I would discover just enough to make me want to know more, and sometimes I would have to speculate and imagine. My ancestors had always been farmers. They were hard workers, but for the most part they were uneducated. They left no letters, no journals, nothing written in their own hands by which I might reconstruct the past. As I was the last of their line, having no children myself, I felt an intense obligation to do what I could to preserve the story of this family in writing.

The fact I began with was this: John A. Martin was born on February 17, 1810, and died on January 2, 1898. I took this information from his tombstone, a tall, narrow monument set upon an impressive slab of granite. The monument spiraled up to an ornamental cornice at its top. Standing before it, I felt a surprisingly strong sense of connection. All those years ago, this man had traveled these same roads, walked through these woodlands and over these prairies, set his plow into the clay soil, listened to quail calling for rain as they were now somewhere behind me. I wanted to know him by more than this monument engraved with his name and the dates upon which he entered and left the world. And then I realized that he was already a part of me; his blood was my blood, something of his spirit mine as well, passed down through generations of Martins. I had spent years thinking myself unlike the Martin men who had farmed this land, and here I was wishing there were some way that I could gather all of them – from John A. to James Henry to Will to my father, Roy – have all of us in a clan.

I left the cemetery and closed the gate, but still the spirit of John A. drifted out and attached itself to me. And what of the Martins who had come before him, names I didn't even know? I felt a great sadness for all the years that separated us, but I was happy, too, that I had discovered John A. I understood that I could put miles of distance between myself and Lukin Township, but family was something I carried with me wherever I went, something more than facts and dates, something, for better or worse, I could never escape.

I found no grave for John A.'s wife that day and no listing later in a book that recorded the dead buried in Lawrence County cemeteries. The description of the Ridgley Cemetery noted that some tombstones either had no names on them or were worn to the point of being unreadable. I wondered whether my great-great-grandmother's was one of those.

"Do you remember her?" I asked Aunt Ferne on a second visit. This time I brought a peck of Red Haven peaches that Deb and I had picked at the orchard.

"Land sakes, no," Aunt Ferne said. "She was dead before I came along."

"What was her name?"

"These peaches are skinned some." Aunt Ferne rubbed her finger over the bruised fruit. "I better sort out the bad and cut them up right now." And with that she went into the kitchen, leaving my question unanswered.

A few days later, in the Lawrenceville Public Library, I found a file of Lawrence County obituaries clipped from local newspapers and mounted on five-by-seven-inch index cards. One of them contained the obituary for Mrs. John A. Martin. Her name was Eliza, and she had died on February 13, 1918, in Tuscola, Illinois, at the age of seventy-one.

I sat in the small room reserved for genealogical research, staring at the date of Eliza's death, 1918. Outside the streets were shimmering with heat. Behind me, in the genealogy room, an oscillating fan turned back and forth on its stand, helping the air conditioning stir the air. A chill came up the back of my neck. I knew that Aunt Ferne had been born on June 4, 1903. She had been nearly fifteen when Eliza Martin died, and yet she had told me that she had no memory of Eliza, that Eliza had been dead at the time of my aunt's birth.

Tuscola was a little over a hundred miles to the north of Sumner, but according to the obituary, on the Friday after Eliza's death, her body had been accompanied to Sumner by her son John D. Martin and his wife and daughter. Funeral services were held that afternoon in the Methodist Church; interment followed in the Ridgley Cemetery.

Why did my aunt, who had recalled with such specificity picking worms from Henry Martin's tobacco plants, had described his rail fences and the crullers Mary Ann made, have no memory of Eliza? And why did Eliza, who had died twenty years after John A., have no tombstone at the Ridgley Cemetery?

All families, I suppose, have secrets; I was about to discover one of ours.

In the biographical section of Eliza's obituary, I learned that her marriage to John A. had been her second. She had first married Edward Phillips in 1862, and she had given birth to five children. Mr. Phillips died in 1871, and in 1874 Eliza married John A. Martin. She would have been twenty-eight; he would have been sixty-four.

Even at that time, when the selection of a spouse was often restricted by geography – families intermarrying again and again because they happened to live near one another – the marriage of Eliza and John A. would have surely been a scandal. And if the thirty-six years' difference in their ages wasn't enough to set people to talking, there had been four children born to their union. Later I would learn that the last, Lula, had been born in 1884, five days prior to John A. Martin's seventy-fourth birthday.

I suspected, of course, that Eliza had been John A.'s second wife, and the Lawrence County census report from 1860 proved this to be true. The report listed John A. Martin and his wife, Elizabeth Gaunce Martin, and six of their eight children; one of them was my great-grandfather, James Henry, sixteen years old at the time. All of the children were listed as having been born in Ohio, true to what my aunt had told me, but in contradiction to what she had said, the census report recorded John A.'s and Elizabeth's places of birth as Kentucky.

Obviously certain stories passed down through the generations had arrived a bit disheveled, rearranged by accident or by will.

But what I knew that day in the public library was that John A. Martin had two wives, Elizabeth Gaunce and Eliza French Phillips. I knew that Eliza was buried in Ridgley Cemetery but that no tombstone marked her grave. What I didn't know was the story of Elizabeth Gaunce, my great-great-grandmother.

By 1870, the next year of the census, she had vanished, as had her daughter Nancy A. John Martin's household contained his sons George, Jackson, and Robert, and his daughter Prudence Louisa (the oldest children, William and Sarah, had married by this time, as had my great-grandfather, James Henry; his firstborn son, my grandfather, Will, was a year old), and two sisters, Ursula and Matilda Fite.

Each fact I found seemed to answer a question while raising another. Between 1860 and 1870, what had happened to Elizabeth and Nancy? Who were Ursula and Matilda Fite, and why were they living with John A. Martin and his four children?

Another look at the obituary file provided some insight into the second question. I found an obituary for Matilda Martin, daughter of Joseph and Malinda Fite, who had come from Ohio by way of Indiana to Lawrence County, Illinois, in March 1869, with her sister. Matilda had married Jackson Martin in 1874, the same year, I couldn't help noting, that his father, John A., had married Eliza

French Phillips. In 1883 Jackson and Matilda and their children moved to Hamilton County, some ninety miles southwest of Lawrence County. One of Matilda's surviving sisters was Ursula Martin. I would later learn that Ursula had married John A.'s youngest son, Robert.

The Lawrence County cemetery book suggested an answer to the first question. In the Brian Cemetery, located a section to the east of the Ridgley Cemetery, there was a grave listed for "Elizabeth, wife of J. W. Martin," and next to it a grave for "Nancy A., daughter of J. W. and E. Martin." Nancy A. died on December 10, 1860, at the age of twenty-one years, one month, eight days. That would mean she was born on November 2, 1839. The 1860 census listing for John A. Martin's family recorded a daughter, Nancy A., twenty years of age. It's quite conceivable that the census was gathered earlier in the year, before her twenty-first birthday.

Elizabeth's date of death was listed as October 17, 1867. Though she was identified as the wife of J. W. Martin instead of J. A., I felt confident that this had been a recorder's error, the etching on the tombstone, perhaps, difficult to read. I was sure that John A. had lost first his daughter Nancy and then his wife, Elizabeth, and had lived a widower seven years before marrying Eliza, a fact my aunt claimed not to know.

I went to see her again; this time Deb and I brought a gift of freshly picked blackberries.

"Oh, these are fat ones," Aunt Ferne said. "I'll keep some out for fresh and use the others in a cobbler."

One of my pleasures that summer was doing kind turns for her – bringing her fresh fruit, taking her out to eat – favors my father would have provided had he been alive. I remember him sharing bushels of apples with her, bringing her corn and tomatoes and beans from his garden. All of this he offered with no thought of receiving anything in return. I wanted to believe that I was as selfless, and in a way, of course, I was. It gave me genuine joy to see my aunt clap her hands together and make a fuss over the peaches and the berries. But in my heart I also knew that each time I came bearing a gift I was trying to bribe her. She knew things about our family, stories I was only beginning to guess, and I wanted to put her at ease, seduce her, so she would feel comfortable telling me everything.

She was a widow living with her son Philip, who had never married, in a rented house on Laurel Street. He had been a sickly child, suffering from infections and seizures, and my aunt had nursed him and kept him close to her all his life. He was a slender man with sloped shoulders and brilliant blue eyes. When he spoke, his voice was sometimes laconic, sometimes rapid and high-pitched with childlike enthusiasm. He told stories about our grandfather's teams of horses, explained how to harvest corn with a shucking peg. And he had a memory for dates. He could recite birthdays, wedding anniversaries, dates of death for various family members. Whatever he had witnessed or whatever someone had told him stuck. Whenever I talked to Aunt Ferne about John A. Martin, Philip kept quiet. Obviously, John A.'s story hadn't survived the generations, or else my cousin was protecting the secret my aunt didn't want known.

When she came back to the living room, having gone into the kitchen to store the berries in the refrigerator, she opened the drapes at the west window, and sunlight streamed into the room. She sat beside me on the sofa, from which we could see the oak tree in her yard.

"Did you ever hear of a Jackson Martin?" I asked her.

"Oh, yes," she said. "Uncle Jack. I remember going to visit him and Aunt Tildie down in Hamilton County."

"Matilda," I said.

"Yes. Aunt Tildie was a Fite. Her and her sister came to live with John Martin after . . ." She bit down on her lip and looked out through the window. "Oh, there's one of my squirrels. Do you see?"

Olney had always been known for its population of albino squirrels, and many of the residents attached feeders to their trees to attract them. The feeders were wooden shelves with skewers that would hold ears of corn. The squirrels could sit on the shelves and help themselves. A white squirrel was at my aunt's feeder. He was sitting on his haunches, reaching up with his front paws to tear kernels from the corncob. He held each kernel and gnawed away at it with his sharp teeth, glancing up with frantic jerks of his head, on guard for the slightest noise or motion that might signal a threat to his bounty. He was eager to get his belly full and then move on.

"After what?" I said to my aunt. "Why did Matilda Fite and her sister come to live with John Martin?"

Aunt Ferne rose and went to the window, keeping her back to me. "He's a greedy one, this one is." She tapped her finger on the glass. "Look at him go at that corn. Like he's starved."

"Matilda's sister's name was Ursula," I said. "I found them in the 1870 census living with John Martin and his children. There was no mention of his wife."

"I told you. His wife died a long time before I was born."

"I found an obituary," I said.

Aunt Ferne laughed. "Oh, I do like to watch these little monkeys. They're full of mischief. Of course some folks think they're a nuisance."

"An obituary," I said again.

Deb was frowning at me. She was shaking her head slowly from side to side, signaling me not to say any more.

Finally Aunt Ferne turned back from the window, and I was surprised to see her face shiny with tears. "The sunshine," she said. "It's so bright it makes my eyes water." She blotted her eyes with her handkerchief. "Now, what were we talking about? Blackberries, yes?"

I left my aunt's house that day ashamed because I had tried to force her to acknowledge a truth she didn't want to admit. I never again raised the subject of John and Eliza, leaving them to my imagination, leaving my aunt to whatever peace she had made with the shame their marriage must have brought to our family.

Facts gathered in subsequent research would suggest a story I was free to construct since my aunt had refused to dictate it with definite information. That had been her gift to me, the license of artistry, though I'm sure she hadn't known it at the time.

Now, nearly ninety-seven, she's lost the power of language. She sits in a wheelchair in the Burgin Nursing Manor, my cousin beside her, patting her hand. She stares straight ahead, doesn't respond to my voice or my touch. Who knows what memories play inside her head? They're hers now, hers alone, and if they're bad, I can't say a word to make them better.

"If you could," I asked her that summer, "would you live your life over?"

"Mercy, no," she told me. "I wouldn't want to see all the suffering."

*

John Martin begins to court Elizabeth Gaunce in the summer of 1833, shortly after the Asiatic cholera has come to Nicholas County. No one knows how to cure it; nothing seems to work – not calomel or powdered mustard seed, not spirits of camphor or snakeroot tea. Most folks believe that the vapors rising from the rotting vegetation in the river bottoms after the spring floods cause the disease. A victim breathes in this miasma, develops the cholera, and by the next day lies dead. Just look at the Hawkins family, who lives on the other side of the Licking River. Already they've lost two children, and it's no wonder, people say, living so close to the river. Lord a mercy.

One evening toward dusk, John and Elizabeth, as has been their habit these past few weeks, sneak off to meet on the ridge that runs between their hollows and follow it toward the river, to a clearing, where they see Mr. Hawkins paddling his skiff across the Licking. On the other side he hefts something from the skiff, and John knows it's the eldest girl, Hannah, that she, too, is dead. In the dim light he can see the way Mr. Hawkins gathers the folds of her dress, the way her head falls back and her long hair fans out. Mr. Hawkins carries her to the spot where he has already buried two others.

"It's Hannah," John says.

"I've got eyes," says Elizabeth, surprised by the sharpness that edges her voice.

Over the years she has listened to stories passed down through generations of Gaunces – "Gons," the name used to be spelled – stories of people dying aboard the ship, the *William and Mary*, that sailed from Rotterdam. "They threw them in the ocean," her father said. "Left them for the fishes. Poor souls. No home for them. Thank heavens your great-great-grandfather was strong."

Elizabeth has grown up listening to stories of death: the dead at sea, the dead at the hands of the Shawnee Indians in Pennsylvania, the dead in the Revolution, the dead from the ruin of childbirth. Her father's first wife, Rachel, died three days after delivering Elizabeth's half-brother, Samuel. There were so many ways to die. And now this, this cholera that seems to lurk in the air. It's too much for her to think how suddenly her life might end. Here's Hannah Hawkins now, lying in a heap on the riverbank, her father digging yet another grave. Just last Saturday Elizabeth saw the two of them at Clarke's gristmill on the Johnston Fork. Hannah was showing off a new ribbon, a pretty red one she had in her black hair. She raised Elizabeth's braid and let it fall as if it were as immaterial as wheat chaff. "Elizabeth, I declare," she said. "Your hair is as dry as straw." Then she shook her head so her own glorious hair shimmered and waved as if it were the sparkling water splashing over the mill wheel. "Someday I'm going to have a comb," she said. "A comb made from ivory, and won't that be fine?"

Now the cholera has taken her. Maybe, Elizabeth thinks, listening to the sound of Mr. Hawkins's shovel, it's vanity that kills us, vanity and greed. Maybe we want too much – we think we deserve more – and God punishes us for not being happy with our lot, with the life he gave us as a blessing.

"I was just saying," says John. "Hannah." He knows he's done something to bother Elizabeth, but he can't say he's sorry because he doesn't know what he should be sorry for.

And Elizabeth can't tell him, can't say that what really troubles her is the fact that she loves him, so desperately loves him, even now when the cholera is in the air, when she thinks it's pride and lust that kill, when Hannah Hawkins made a show of her hair and dreamed of an ivory comb to adorn it and now lies dead. Still Elizabeth wants him, wants him more than ever, wants him enough to risk these trips toward the river just so the two of them can be alone. She can't bear herself for being so desirous. She's dying for him, she thinks, and can't stop herself.

"Hush," she says. "Don't say anything. Not another word."

For the first time she kisses him. She throws her arms around his neck and pulls his face down to hers. She thinks of the Palatine Germans tossed from ships; the settlers scalped in the Pennsylvania wilderness; the soldiers in the Revolution, their hearts ripped open with musket balls; the women, their insides rotten from babies; Hannah Hawkins taken by the cholera. And here she stands, her arms around John Martin, her lips pressed to his, this man she loves so much it frightens her.

Finally she pulls away, and John sees that she's crying. He feels her tears on his cheeks.

"I have to go now," she says in a choked voice. "I'm sorry. I have to." And then she turns and runs along the ridge. John watches her until she slips down the hills into a hollow and is gone.

He turns back in time to see Mr. Hawkins ease Hannah down into the shallow grave. John waits for some sound of his mourning – a cry, a wail, a curse – but Mr. Hawkins merely sets to his task, his shovel scraping dirt back into the grave. John squats on his haunches, weighted down with all that's happened this eve: Hannah Hawkins dead; Elizabeth sharp with him and then a tearful kiss; and back at home his father, who told him at supper, "My life ain't yours to run. You go on and make shit of your own if you're a mind to, and keep your nose out of mine."

The only Martin listed on the 1810 Nicholas County census is James. He is somewhere between the ages of twenty-six and forty-five; his wife is somewhere between sixteen and twenty-six. They have two sons, each of them younger than ten, as my great-great-grandfather, born in July of that year, would have been at the time the census was taken, November. The 1820 census shows no record of James Martin, but he could have been listed on page 105, which is missing, or he could be the James whose last name is undecipherable. The age of that James, and the ages of his wife and children, make it possible that this is the James Martin family from the 1810 census. James Martin appears again in the 1830 census, and again, considering the ten years that have passed since the last counting, the family members fall into the appropriate age ranges. Although I can't be sure that this James Martin is my great-great-great-grandfather – the father of John A. Martin – there's a good likelihood that he is. And what stuns me, when I look at that 1830 report, is the fact that this James Martin owned one male slave, age twenty-four to thirty-six.

I've always thought that my ancestors would have lacked the wealth and affluence that would have made it possible for them to be slaveholders. Although the Martins have always been landowners, everything I know about my father and grandfather and great-grandfather tells me that they were always landowners of modest means, content to work their small acreages through their own sweat. Therefore, when I used to imagine the Martins in Kentucky in the early 1800s, I always pictured large families toiling in their fields, getting by, moving to Ohio and later to Illinois in search of better land, more opportunity, the pot of gold always out of reach beyond the rainbow. This narrative, I must admit, always appealed to me because I like to think that hard work and decent living produce their own reward by strengthening the character of those who have to struggle. Perhaps I'm romanticizing the working-class life, but I've known enough farmers and factory workers, and was for a time one of them myself, to know that many of them possess a decency and honesty that lend them a certain measure of integrity.

So it's difficult for me to accept that one of my ancestors owned a slave. Only one, I might say, and try to make this more palatable. But to me that number makes the fact even more shameful, makes me believe that James Martin bought that slave not because he really needed him for the farm work – after all, James had three sons to help him – but simply because he had the money to spend – and wouldn't his neighbors take note (the Gaunces, the Earlywines, the Fites) when they saw that he was the first of the farmers along the Johnston Fork who could afford to buy his labor just like the uppity planters who had come from Virginia?

Some years back, before he had made his way with his own place, he had gone to one of those planters, a Mr. Buckner, to ask for work. Mr. Buckner was astride a walking horse with the daintiest saddle James had ever seen. He had to shade his eyes with his hand and look up into the sun shining behind Mr. Buckner, who wore a tall silk hat the color of red wine and held a riding crop in his gloved hand. "What's wrong with you, boy?" Mr. Buckner laughed. "Don't you know I've got niggers to work my fields?"

James has never forgotten the shame that came over him. Mr. Buckner's horse reared up, his front hooves pawing at the air, and James stumbled back out of the way. Then Mr. Buckner reined the horse and whipped him across the withers with his crop before cantering off to his fields, where his slaves, a passel of them, were hoeing corn.

John doesn't know any of this. All he knows is how often he's seen coffles of slaves, handcuffed and chained, drivers lashing them with whips when their shuffling steps slowed, moving them along the Maysville Road toward the auction block. One day one of the slaves, a young man with a broad chest and powerful arms, caught John's eye, looked at him with such heat that John hated Kentucky, hated himself for living there, hated his father, who had already started to talk of buying "a good, strong buck."

"I'll work harder," John tells him when he comes home after watching Mr. Hawkins bury Hannah. "Whatever needs doing, I'll see to it." He remembers how Mr. Hawkins didn't utter a sound as he set to his work. There was only the ring of his shovel working the rocky ground, the call of an owl somewhere back in the hollow. The horrible things people could get used to. It amazes John and sickens him, too. "I'll work the tobacco," he says. "Daybreak to sundown. Please, Pa."

I'm making my protest John's, filling him with the disgust I hope I would have felt had I been the one with a father who proposed to buy a slave at auction. But in another time and place, who's to say how I would have reacted? It's so easy to be virtuous, courageous, from a distance of time and space.

But John's here, in 1833, alone with his father at nightfall at the oak stump they use for a chopping block. James has just finished splitting wood. He drives the ax into the block and lets the blade stick there. "No one says you have to go along."

John says again what he said to his father at supper. "It's wrong what you're wanting to do." Then adds: "Weren't we Quakers – the Martins, I mean – when we came from Ireland?"

"Them was different times. Now we're Methodists."

"And it's all right to buy another man? Force him to work your fields?"

"I'll give him food and clothes. I'll treat him same as I treat you."

"Me? I could leave here anytime I take a mind to."

"Leave, would you?" James laughs and slaps his hand against his leg. "Where in the world would you go?"

"Somewhere different than Kentucky. I'll tell you that. It's a dirty shame, what you're thinking. I wouldn't want it on my soul."

"Is it your good Quaker conscience talking?" James pauses, pitches his voice lower. "Or is all this bluster on account of you're afraid of what Elizabeth will say, afraid she might take up with another spark? You see, I know all about what you're up to. You ain't as secret as you think. What's that the good book says about casting the first stone?"

He leaves John to stand alone in the dark, to wonder whether what his father's said is true. What did Mr. Hawkins do when, finally, he had covered Hannah with dirt? John likes to think that the night breeze blowing across the river chilled him, sweat-soaked as he was from his labor, that he began to tremble and shiver, suddenly as cold as he had ever been. Perhaps it was then that he cried – while Elizabeth was running along the ridge, while John was tromping along the same path, while there was no one to bear witness to Mr. Hawkins paddling his skiff back across the river to tell his wife the chore was done.

Because my father had no hands, he sometimes hired men to help him on our farm. My mother was as much help as she could be – driving grain trucks, greasing machinery, doctoring cattle and hogs – and my father could do many of the tasks that he had been able to perform before his accident. He could drive our International H tractor, plowing and disking and harrowing our fields. He could drive a combine and a corn picker at harvest time. But still there was work that neither he nor my mother could manage – baling hay, making certain repairs to machinery – and, when that was the case, my father paid someone to do the chore. I remember a succession of such men, hay hands and mechanics – jacks of all trades – men who weren't prosperous and had to scrabble from odd job to odd job. I never knew who to feel more sorry for, the men who had to hire themselves out or my father, whose handicap forced him to rely on their skills.

He always treated the hired men well, paid them whatever they asked, and insisted that they stay for a meal. Before they sat at our table, they washed their faces and hands at our basin and left my mother's towels streaked with oil and grease and grime. They rolled up their sleeves until the white flesh of their biceps showed. They took off their caps, and their foreheads were pale. These men were timid as my father encouraged them to eat more chicken, more potatoes, more bread. "You worked a ton," he said. "You need to get your belly full."

I was always surprised at how shy the hired men were at our table, how humble, how hesitant, despite my father's urging, to help themselves to seconds and thirds. These men, who had wrestled hay bales, yanked on wrenches, cursed stubborn nuts and bolts, were like children at our table, and my father, who was so often angry with me, was genuinely pleased to have them gathered there. I was happy, too, because as long as the men were there, I felt protected from my father. In their presence his temper lay dormant the way thistles and horseweed and wild garlic died back at frost. On the days when the hired men came into our house, I wished that my father could always be as relaxed, as jolly, as he was then.

But eventually the men would leave, drive up our lane in rattletrap cars or trucks, and sooner or later I would do something to irritate my father, and he would pull off his belt and use it to lash me. I would wish that I had some skill like those men, something that my father couldn't do without, something that would make him treat me more kindly.

I wonder now whether he enjoyed hosting the hired men only because he was grateful and wanted to show them how much he appreciated all they had done – our barn's loft stacked with bales of clover hay, hydraulic leaks repaired on our tractor – or whether it also satisfied him to make a display of his charity, to tap his hook against a meat platter and tell someone, "Dig in. Don't be bashful. If you go away hungry, you've got no one to blame but yourself."

How desperately he must have wanted to be one of them, a whole man, free from those hooks and the stumps of his arms, which he slipped into the hooks' hard plastic holsters. Each day he must have wished to be rid of the harness of canvas straps, the cable wires, the thick bands made of rubber, the ache in his shoulders where he contracted his muscles to tug at the wires, stretch the bands, and open the hooks. I wonder whether he ever dreamed himself whole again, his hands agile and strong, and whether, in those dreams, he touched me with tenderness. I can't imagine what it would have been like had he been able to do that. I only knew the cold steel of his hooks, the prickly cable wires, the snap of those pincers as they sprang shut.

During recess at school we often played Red Rover. Two lines of children, human chains formed by spacing ourselves just far enough apart so we could grasp the hand of the classmates to our left and right, faced each other across some twenty feet of playground. One line called out to the other: "Red Rover, Red Rover. Send Bobby right over." The person called ran toward the opposite chain and tried to break through. I always hoped that Katrina and I would be on the same team. When we were, I tried to arrange it so we were next to each other. I loved the feel of her hand in mine. If an opponent dashed toward our link in the chain, I held her hand as tightly as I could, determined not to feel it slip from my grasp.

In those days I was starved for tactile sensations, and Katrina, with whom I shared a double desk in our classroom, was the source of so much that pleased me: the warmth of her hand, the soft fuzz of her angora sweater, the airy billow of her empress sleeves. Sometimes, when we were at her house, we rode her horse, Lightning. I sat in the saddle behind Katrina, my arms wrapped around her waist. I was often secretly frightened by Lightning's gallop, but delighted, too, because Katrina and I were so close. I was determined not to let her know that I was afraid.

Elizabeth has always dreamed that one day she and John will marry, but on the night she comes back from the clearing where they watched Mr. Hawkins bury Hannah, she fears that it's been an omen, a sign that her love for John is a malady, a sickness that will consume her if she doesn't put an end to it.

Her father and mother are entertaining a visitor inside their log house. From the light of the blaze in the kitchen fireplace, Elizabeth can see that the visitor is the preacher, Michael Geoghegan. She recognizes his muttonchop sideburns and his labored breathing. He clasps his hands together on his stomach. The fire snaps and sparks. Someone like him, she thinks. That's who she should marry. Someone she doesn't care a twig about, an old bachelor who must think any chance he's ever had at love has come and gone. She would never feel prideful of him. With him she would be thankful for small pleasures. God would never accuse her of being greedy or vain.

"Reverend," she says. She comes up behind him and lets her hand rest on his shoulder. "It's Elizabeth."

He half turns, trying to catch a glimpse of her, but he can hardly manage to shift his weight about on the narrow seat of the rocking chair. She sees the sweat leaking from the bramble of his sideburns, smells a harsh odor – a mix of tallow and salt – rising from his skin. He reaches up awkwardly, since his arms are short, and lays his hand over hers. She's surprised at how dry it is, how cool. "Elizabeth," he says. "Dear Elizabeth. I was hoping you'd come before I had to take my leave."

Take my leave. How high-heel, she thinks. She tries to convince herself it's an elegant thing to say. "If you'll be so good to excuse me, I simply must take my leave." But really it sounds so silly and out of place, the way Michael Geoghegan himself often seems there in the hills and hollows of Nicholas County, wearing vest and hammertail coat in even the hottest weather.

"Sit down, Elizabeth," her mother says. She's sitting close to the fire, carding wool. The gentle ripping sound is like the sound a brush makes through Elizabeth's hair. "Stay with us awhile. We were talking about this horrible cholera."

"Yes, Elizabeth." Michael Geoghegan pats her hand. "Please stay."

Elizabeth wants nothing more than to climb up to the loft where Prudence and Moses and Zed are already asleep and to go to sleep herself and forget for a time that she loves her cousin John. Even though it's not uncommon for cousins to marry, her lust for him shames her. Would a good Christian girl have such thoughts? She wants too much too fast, and she fears she'll be the next one that the cholera takes.

"Michael was just telling us the most amazing story." Elizabeth's father is paring an apple; the red peel curls in a long twist from his knife. "Tell it again, Michael. Say it so Elizabeth can hear it. A miracle if I ever heard tell."

George Gaunce is a man who believes in miracles, believes in the glory of God's grace, and Elizabeth knows she can't disappoint him now that he's invited Michael Geoghegan to again tell his story. How rude it would be for her to make some feeble excuse and then scurry away. She pulls up a cane-bottom chair and sits between her father and Michael Geoghegan, in front of the fire that they keep burning year-round, no matter the heat, because if it ever goes cold, it's such a bother to light again, the backlog having to be dragged to the house with a horse and then brought in on rollers, a shovel of fire borrowed from a neighbor, covered with dry ashes, and toted home.

"I was just up to the Williams place," Michael Geoghegan says, settling into the somber intonation he uses on Sundays when he preaches his sermons. "Poor Mrs. Williams laying corpse in her pine box. The cholera. Mr. Williams was grieving, stroking her hand, her face, saying her name over and over in a whisper. And then all of a sudden he looked at me, and he said, 'Michael, I swear I just felt her finger move.' I thought he must be dreaming it or that it was only the body's muscles stiffening. But then I looked down at poor Mrs. Williams, and there was her forefinger waggling about." He pauses, and for a while the only sound is his breathing and the crackle of the fire. Even Elizabeth's mother, though she has already heard this story, has stopped carding wool. When Michael Geoghegan speaks again, his voice is hushed. "Do you know what happened next?" he asks Elizabeth.

"No, what?" she says. Her heart is pounding the way it does in church when Michael Geoghegan speaks of the individual's responsibility for eternal happiness. Grace is universal. All one has to do is choose the light, walk on the side of good, act as one with Christ. "Save yourself," he often exhorts. "No one is ever truly lost." Elizabeth scoots to the edge of her chair. She leans toward Michael Geoghegan. "Tell me," she says. "What happened?"

"Mrs. Williams sat up in her casket." Michael Geoghegan's voice rises in pitch and deepens in timbre. He reaches his arms out in front of him as if he were once again beholding Mrs. Williams. "She . . . sat . . . up," he says slowly, stressing each word, so precious they are, so wondrous the sight. "Sat up," he says again. "Praise God."

Most of the night, as she lies awake in the loft, Elizabeth marvels over the story of Mrs. Williams and how she could hear her husband grieving, was conscious all the time, but had to work up the strength to move. So close to death, and then . . . Elizabeth pictures again and again Mrs. Williams sitting up in her casket. The idea of it makes Elizabeth's heart glad, makes her believe in second chances. We can almost be lost, she thinks, and yet somehow find our way back. She says a prayer in her head. "Please, God, forgive me my sins." She can't bring herself to name them one by one: the wicked thoughts she had about Hannah Hawkins the day at the gristmill when she showed off her lovely hair; the fact that she, Elizabeth, has kissed her cousin John this very evening; that she has dreamed of his nakedness, dreamed of having him the way God meant a wife and husband to have each other. I'll go to sleep, she thinks, and in the morning, when I wake, all those feelings for John will be gone. The day will be new, and so will I. I'll jump right up, and I'll do like Michael Geoghegan says: I'll walk toward the light.

But the morning is dark and damp with drizzle. Mist rises from the hills; low clouds gather above the hollows. The rain drips down as Elizabeth, an apron held over her head, hurries out to the smoke-house to fetch a hunk of bacon. She pushes open the smokehouse door and steps inside quickly to get out of the rain. And there, step-ping from the shadows, head ducked to avoid the hams and bacons and loins hooked and hanging from hickory withes, is John.

"Lizzie." He takes her hands. "Oh, Liz," he says. "I've been out half the night."

"You've been out in the rain." Water still drips from his face. She wipes it with her apron. "Look at you. You're soaked to the bone."

"I aimed to run off." His voice is shaking. "But I couldn't. Not 'til I came for you."

"Run off? What kind of foolishness is that?"

"I can't stay here. Not the way Pa's acting." John pulls Elizabeth to him and hugs her against his wet body. She can smell the river on him, a rotten smell of fish and mud. "He's going to Carlisle this morning, Lizzie. To the slave auction." Elizabeth feels John shivering. "To buy a slave, Lizzie. I can barely say the word."

Something passes, then, from John's shivering body into hers. She can feel it, his fervor, and she realizes this is what she loves about him, this passion he has, the way he can feel so deeply. And, at the same time, it's what she fears, this ardor that can put him off his head, make him do something mad.

"Run off," she says again. She strokes his cheek. "Oh, John." She tries to calm him. "Our homes are here. Our families."

"Family," he says with disgust. Then he pushes her away from him and runs out into the rain.

Once, on a rainy afternoon, Katrina and Dan and I were in their basement playing a game of *Sorry.* Dan and I were sitting cross-legged on the cool cement floor; Katrina was lying on her stomach, propped up on her elbows. I felt cozy there in the dry basement, looking up from time to time at the rain-blurred windows above us. It was raining, as my father would have said, "like pouring piss out of a boot." I could hear the rainwater gushing from the down-spouts and puddling in the dirt. The thunderclaps were muffled and sounded far away because we were underground, insulated and dry, protected from the storm. We rolled our dice and moved our pieces over the game board, and the easy rhythm we fell into – the dice clicking, the tokens thumping – pleased me.

Then Dan started to pester Katrina. He was sitting next to her, and he kept pinching her leg. "Skeeters are out," he kept saying. "Bsst! There's another one."

Katrina squirmed about and slapped at his hand. "Quit it, Dan."

"I'm not doing anything," he said. "It's those skeeters."

Because I was an only child, I had no knowledge of the give and take between siblings. I knew nothing about their rivalries and affections. When I saw Dan pinching Katrina – when I took note of her mounting anger – I thought I understood perfectly: Dan was the villain; Katrina was his innocent victim, a damsel in distress.

Now, when I remember Dan, I call to mind a slight boy, so much smaller than other boys his age. "He's the runt of that litter," my father always said.

And it was true. Dan, who was three years older than I, was perhaps an inch shorter. His brothers were both tall and beefy, but Dan was elfish, a sprout yet to take root and grow. I imagine now that he must have resented those of us who were younger. Even though he was generally good-humored and friendly (in fact, I can recall several times when he defended me against the teasing of older boys), surely, anytime we had to assume a line at school, he must have grown tired of always having to join the first-graders (here he is in our class photo, sitting cross-legged on the floor with the rest of the pipsqueaks, while his chums, the fourth-graders, loom over us) or, at Christmastime, of having to be one of Santa's pint-sized helpers in the school pageant.

I wonder, too, if perhaps he resented Katrina because she was the only girl in the family, a good-hearted child who claimed everyone's attention. Maybe that's why he was pestering her in the basement on that rainy afternoon. Or maybe he was pinching Katrina's leg because he loved her deeply and couldn't say it, could only show it with a gesture that he considered playful and harmless. Or maybe he was just bored, frustrated with the rain that kept us confined to the basement.

I didn't understand, then, the complicated crosscurrents that run through a family's affections, though eventually I would figure out that even in my father's anger, and my anguish as a result of it, lay a wellspring of genuine love. Why else would we have been so disappointed with each other, so ashamed after an ugly scene? Why else would we have longed for a life more considerate and kind?

All I knew that day in the basement was that Katrina didn't like what Dan was doing to her anymore than I liked their terrier nipping at my ankles.

"Leave her alone," I said. I shoved at Dan's shoulder, momentarily knocking him off balance.

"I'm not hurting her," he said, when he had regained his balance. Then he shoved me back. "Don't be a baby."

I don't remember exactly what happened next, only that we were wrestling. On Saturday nights my father let me stay up late so we could watch *Championship Wrestling* together on channel seven. It was one of the few times I felt close to him, both of us rooting for Rip Hawk or Dick the Bruiser. It seems ironic to me now, but perhaps natural, too, in a perverse way, that we would unite as spectators of violence, staged as it most surely was, when so many times my father had left stripes on my skin with his belt. Watching the wrestling matches, I learned holds and moves: the hammerlock, the headlock, the body scissors, the reverse toe hold, the abdominal stretch, the flying mule kick.

I believe it was the headlock that I eventually used on Dan that day in the basement, and somehow in his attempt to escape it, he fell back and banged his head on the cement floor.

It's difficult to ever forget the sound of a skull hitting concrete, especially when you in some way are to blame for it. I stood over Dan, stunned. He lay motionless for a moment. Then he sat up, sheepishly rubbing his head, looking dazed.

"You hurt him." Katrina was drumming her fists into my back. I spun around, surprised, and she hit me in the chest. "You're awful," she said, and then, as if she never wanted to have anything to do with me, she ran up the stairs, leaving Dan and me alone.

"Are you all right?" I asked him.

"Yeah, I'm okay."

I felt such an emptiness inside, similar to the sinking sensation I got riding in a car that crested a hill too fast and dipped down the other side. "Hold onto your gizzard," my mother always said. I wondered whether this emptiness was what my father felt after he had whipped me, sorry that he had let his temper get the better of him, sorry that he had gone too far, sorry that the world he thought he had a hold on had slipped out from under him.

John runs up the slope of the hollow toward the ridge. He runs through the rain, trying to convince himself that he can keep going. He'll find the Maysville Road and set out for Ohio. He doesn't know what he'll do once he gets there – hire out as a farm hand maybe – but at least he'll be far away from his father, far away from Elizabeth, who has refused him. That moment in the smokehouse, when she stroked his cheek, embarrasses him. It was as if she thought him a crackbrain or a child, incapable of knowing what was right.

As he climbs the slope, sapling branches whip by him. He holds his arms out to part them. He's shivering from the cold and the damp, and suddenly he feels more alone than he ever has. And what surprises him is the fact that he finds himself yearning for his father even though he has tried his best to despise him: his father, who evenings asks John's mother to read him a piece from the Bible, who used to carve dolls out of gourds and leave them for John's sisters to find. That was before his fingers stiffened and curled from years of farm work – years of clearing stumps, stripping sorghum, shucking corn, cradling wheat, setting tobacco plants. John has worked alongside him, has done so gladly, has imagined that he would continue to do so for some time to come.

But now everything has changed. John's father is on his way to buy a slave, a deed John abhors even more now that Elizabeth has failed to share his outrage. "I'll show her," he says aloud, and his voice sounds strange to him – hoarse and tear-choked – so strange that it seems to come from someone he doesn't know, and he realizes this someone is the foul part of himself, the part that is capable of spleen. He has tried to hate his father, has tried to hate Elizabeth. But he has only succeeded in hating himself because he now knows that his outrage over his father's intent to buy a slave hasn't been, as he has wanted to believe, noble and born from love, but instead from something base and selfish, a desire for self-protection, a fear that, as his father suggested, Elizabeth might turn away from him, that he might lose her to another.

A branch lashes him across the cheek, and he feels the blood run down to his mouth. The taste stops him cold, the warm rust of it, reminding him of a time he saw a slave whipped on the Maysville Road, a young girl who had crumpled to her knees, too tired to keep walking. Each wrist was tied to that of a woman who walked beside her, and when she fell to the ground, the whole line of slaves came to a halt. The driver brought his whip down across the girl's back, but she stayed down. He told the two women who were tied to her to "heft her up and drag her along." And they did.

John pants and pants, doubled over, his hands on his knees. Then he straightens and heads off in the direction of home.

Once, at a family Christmas gathering, someone proposed a showing of home movies. How grand! I must have been around ten years old, and I lived in a house where the few snapshots that my mother took came from a camera borrowed from my aunt. To see my relatives, maybe even me at an earlier age, moving about on the movie screen was about the most delightful thing I could imagine.

But before the show could get under way, one of my uncles pointed out that my father would be in the movies – my father before his accident, when he still had his hands. "I don't think Lee should see that," my uncle said in a low voice he didn't mean for me to hear. But I did, and immediately I felt the excitement drain from the afternoon. I also felt a touch of shame at being the object of pity. I was aware of being outside the family by virtue of my father's circumstances, loved all the same, but not allowed to fully participate for fear some harm might come to me.

Now I would give up practically anything to see those movies, even to have seen them then so I would have their images in my mind, images of my father and his hands. I imagine him now in the slightly jerky frames of the film. Perhaps he's sitting at a kitchen table, snapping down cards with a flourish as he takes a trick in a game of pitch. I can see his gold wedding band catch the light and glint. After all the cards are played, he snaps his fingers and pops his palm against his fist, that timeless good-guy gesture that says everything's aces. Or maybe he's outside on a sunny afternoon, putting on some silly face for the camera. He's juggling three oranges. Then I'm there, crawling across the grass. He catches the oranges and stuffs them into his jacket pockets. He scoops me up in his hands, lifts me above his head, raises me toward the sky. Perhaps if I had watched those home movies, I would have seen that my father had once been a happier man. Maybe I would have understood that the accident had changed him, filled him with rage. Maybe something significant would have happened for both of us that Christmas. We might have learned to be more tolerant, to humble ourselves before the horrible things that could happen in a life to change it forever.

The slave's name is Luke, and James Martin buys him for four hundred dollars. Luke knows how much four hundred dollars is. He can count money, and he can read because his former owner, Mrs. Maudie Taylor of Maysville, schooled him. Poor Missus Taylor, dead now from the cholera and everyone from her house sold at auction: Starr, the house girl; Aunt Bell, the washwoman; and him, Luke, the yardman. How he misses the grand gardens he tended, bright and fragrant with roses, hollyhocks, gladiolus, moonflowers. And the orchards: the peach trees and apple trees, the blackberry canes and strawberry beds. He imagines them growing up in weeds, fruit rotting on the ground, and for that reason alone he wants to cry.

But he won't. Not here. He makes his face a stone and watches the clerk tell his new owner, "James Martin, you sign your name right here."

He points to a line on the bill, but James hesitates. He bows his head. "I can't," he says in a low voice. "Never learned my letters."

"Can't write your name?" the clerk says. "All right then. I'll sign it for you, and then you make an X above it. You can manage that, can't you?"

"Yes, sir. I reckon I can."

Luke forms the letters in his head while Mister James scratches an X on the bill, making his mark. Luke knows he could sign that name in a whipstitch, *James*, and make it come out as pretty as you please. Knowing that – holding it as a secret inside him – somehow makes this all a touch more tolerable. He holds his shoulders back, keeps his head level. He stands ramrod straight, the way he did the few times Missus Taylor permitted him to serve at table.

"Well, James Martin," the clerk says, blotting the ink dry. "You've done bought yourself this boy."

"Yes, sir." James studies the bill of sale. He holds it close to his face.

Then he folds it carefully and puts it in the pocket of his britches.

"Go on then," the clerk says. "Take him home. 'Less, of course," he chuckles, "you expect to do some more buying today."

"No, I'm done," James says. "I got what I come for."

He turns to Luke, and for a good while he doesn't say a word, only stares, and Luke understands that he can't get it into his head how he's supposed to act now that he owns a man. Part of Luke takes joy in the fact that Mister James is so balled up, and yet another part of him wants to do something to be of help. He can see the clerk still chuckling, well-aware that Mister James is ill-bred for this sort of thing.

Finally Luke does the only thing he can think to do. He takes a small step toward Mister James, a step barely perceptible, but it's enough to unfreeze him. James points off to the west, where buggies with their fine horses are tied to the hitching rails around the court-house square. "Reckon we'll go then," he says. "Come on, Luke. Wagon's over yonder."

The rickety flatbed wagon, meant for hauling, not for show, looks out of place among the buggies with their tassel-trimmed canopies. Mister James's horse is swaybacked, its hooves and pasterns speckled with mud.

Luke follows Mister James, noticing the way he walks with a stoop, his back all humped up. His trousers are linsey-woolsey, homespun the same as Luke's own.

"Don't they make a pair?" the clerk says as they leave the court-house lawn. "Martin and his boy."

From time to time, in public, I had to help my father with a task. In stores I took his billfold from his shirt pocket and, at his instruction, fished out the appropriate bills and coins to settle our accounts. In the barber shop, if it was winter, I helped him off with his coat and cap. After our haircuts, he sometimes tried to open the shop's door, and his hook, the pincers spread wide to close around the knob, locked into that position. He couldn't turn the knob or let go of it. "I'm fast," he would say to me then, humbled by his inadequacy, and I would have to pry back one of the pincers so he could free himself.

I always felt that I was on display whenever he called on me to do something he couldn't. "Roy, who's your helper?" someone might say to him.

"That's my boy," he would say, and despite all the trouble between us, there would be an affectionate lilt to his voice, and I would believe that in his heart of hearts, where he was whole and without temper or regret, he loved me.

"He looks like a good helper," someone would say, and my father would answer, "Well, sure he is. He's my right-hand man."

I would forget, then, the whippings he had given me, would convince myself that there wouldn't be any others, that we were moving into a better part of our lives. I was his helper, his right-hand man. That was my job.

Then one summer there came a time when I could do nothing to help him. A fisherman had drowned in the Jents' pond. He had leaned out too far to reel in a catch and had fallen from his boat. He had sunk to the bottom and never come up.

The first we knew of it was when his buddy, a skinny boy, gasping for air, came to our door begging for help. It was toward evening, the sun a reddish orange ribbon in the west, just beginning to sink below the horizon. Water ran from the boy and puddled on our front porch. He had dove and dove, he told us, hoping to find his buddy, but had come up empty-handed.

"Mister," he said to my father. "Please. You've got to do something."

What could my father do but turn to other men for help? He told my mother to call the sheriff and then Mack Jent.

Earlier that summer, when a mountain lion had been killing livestock, a group of men at the Berryville Store had formed a hunting party and gone out with rifles. My father had gone with them, a bundle of rope looped over his shoulder, looking ineffectual among the men and their guns.

The evening the boy came to tell us his buddy had fallen into the pond, I got the same feeling that had come over me the night my father marched off with the men: a tender pity for him and all he lacked. He would never be the one that people could depend on in a time of crisis. He would never shoot a mountain lion, never rescue a drowning man. He would never be Lucas McCain from *The Rifle-*

man, or Paladin from *Have Gun, Will Travel*, television characters who always saved the day.

What made me especially sad was the knowledge that inside my father *was* that kind of man – decisive, resourceful, courageous – and that had he only had hands he would have been better able to demonstrate those qualities. He would have been freed from the clumsy movements of his hooks. How many times had he mourned a physical action he once performed with ease, now lost to him forever?

That evening, as dusk gathered, he could only stand on the bank of the Jents' pond while Mack and his oldest boy, David, and the skinny boy went out in the rowboat and dropped a tangle of barbed wire, tied to a rope, down into the water. They hoped that the barbed wire would snag the drowned man's clothing and then the three of them might be able to haul the body to the surface.

I stood beside my father as the dark came on. I could hear the boat moving on the pond, the oars creaking in their locks, the paddles slapping the water.

Then Mack shouted, "I think we've got something."

My father said to me, "You go on home. You don't need to be here to see this."

I wonder now whether he was thinking of the moment when a farmer driving past my father's field heard his cries for help and freed him from the corn picker, brought him from the field, his hands mangled to pulp.

"I'll stay with you," I said. I wonder how long he stood in the field, his hands caught in the rollers of the picker's shucking box, before the other farmer happened by.

"You do like I say." My father's voice was angry now. "Or do you want me to blister your ass?"

I ran across the field toward the lights burning in our farmhouse. I was crying because I had to leave my father there, alone in the dark – helpless. All he could do was wait while Mack and David and the skinny boy pulled the drowned man from the pond.

Last year I went to Burgin's Nursing Home to visit Aunt Ferne and my cousin Philip. Aunt Ferne lay in bed, blind and unable to speak.

Philip received me in the nursing home's lobby, where a glass-cased aviary contained brilliantly colored songbirds. They flitted about the silk greenery, poked their heads out of straw-colored nests. Philip still had his talent for recalling the dates of family births, marriages, and deaths. He could also retrieve the most trivial details: the makes and years of cars people had driven, street addresses, appliance brands, the names of pets long gone. Even at the age of seventy-three, his mind was still sharp.

I asked him whether he remembered our grandfather, Will Martin, who died in 1941, when Philip was fifteen and my birth lay fourteen years in the future. I hoped that he could tell me something about our grandfather that would help me better understand my father and our difficult relationship.

Philip nodded his head. "Oh, sure. I remember Grandpa." Philip still had the bright blue eyes of a child. "He had horses. He had Dolly and Dan and Prince, and . . ."

I listened to every name, more names than I would ever be able to hold in my head. "Was he anything like my dad?" I said when Philip finally took a breath.

"Oh, I reckon. Sure, I guess." Philip looked off toward the aviary, his eyes following the swoop of a bird with orange feathers on its chest. Then he turned his gaze back to me, and he gave me a fact I never could have predicted, a detail that stunned me with its irony. "One of Grandpa's hands was sort of twisted." Philip spread the fingers of his right hand and held it, clawlike, on his knee. "Then your dad got his hands in that corn picker."

I wanted to stop him. I wanted to know why Will Martin's hand was deformed. In the only photograph I have of him that shows his hands, he's sitting on a chair, his hands resting on his legs. I had always thought that the right one appeared to be cramped up just because he hadn't relaxed it. But when I study the photograph now, after my visit with Philip, it's clear that the fingers are cramped up because the hand is turned, the wrist joint deformed to the point that he can't let his hand lie flat on his leg. My father had rarely spoken of his father, and, when he had, he had never said a word about his deformed hand.

When I was a child, I would sit in the Church of Christ and occasionally witness at the end of the service a member who had fallen astray go to the front of the congregation during the invitation call. Almost always, this man or woman would be weeping. When the singing stopped, the preacher always announced that a lost child had come home. I remember the feeling I had at those moments – such awe that the person had come forward to make their wrongs public, such admiration, such love for the weakness of people and the strength. I always felt a little sorry for them, too, having to stand there, sobbing, faces shiny with tears, shoulders heaving. Then the preacher asked them whether they wished to rededicate their lives to Christ, and they nodded, and that would be enough to put an ache in my throat – that gentle movement, that *yes*.

"Yes," we all seemed to be saying after the service, when we rushed to the ones who had been lost. We shook their hands. We hugged them to us. We welcomed them back to the fold, their coming forward – their confession – bringing us all closer because we weren't so different, all of us vulnerable, imperfect, but together for the time, doing the best we could with our lives and the stories we couldn't stop them from telling.

In the nursing home Philip told a story about our grandfather's horses, a story passed down to him. It was a few months after my father was born, in 1913, and Will Martin and his brother-in-law, Dave Hill . . . "That was Ida's husband," Philip says. "Our Grandma Stella's sister. There was Idie and Stellie and Laurie and Della and Fannie and Nellie, and the three boys, Elmer, and John, and Fred." Philip counted them off on his fingers and then went on with his story about Dave Hill and Will Martin each plowing with a team of horses one evening when a storm came up and lightning struck Dave Hill. "Grandpa came a tearing up the lane. Driving that team of horses. It was Dolly and Prince. The buckles on their harness were jingling to beat the band."

Suddenly I wasn't listening. I was imagining the night when Dave Hill lay dead in the field and Will Martin drove his team of horses wildly up the lane, carrying the news. Later, when Dave Hill's body had been carried to the mortuary, and Ida had been comforted, and it was quiet in the house, the rainstorm now only a sound of wet leaves dripping, a scent of clean air, a chill on the wind, did Will Martin find himself bent over my father's cradle? It's the story I prefer: my grandfather thinking how lucky he is to be alive; my father sleeping sweetly, absolved from all that's yet to come. Perhaps he even wakes, reaches out, and Will Martin touches him, amazed by how small each finger is, how perfect, how different from his own.

I leave them there, Will Martin petting his son, touching him ever so shyly with his twisted hand, on this night when death has come and they have both survived.

It's stopped raining by the time James and Luke leave Carlisle, and James is sorry because, if the rain were still coming down, it would be easy to hunker down inside himself and forget that Luke is sitting behind him in the wagon. Now, with the sun starting to break through the clouds, with the wind calm and the day turning fair, James feels obliged to make conversation but isn't sure it would be proper. He has to admit to himself that he doesn't know how to behave around Luke. He doesn't know whether to speak to him sternly or with kindness. They travel a good ways up the Saltwell Road before he says anything at all.

"I don't have much of a place," he says, surprised at how easily he admits this to Luke. "A few acres of tobacco, some corn. I keep a few pigs and hogs. A milk cow. Some chickens."

"Yes, sir," Luke says.

"You ever worked tobacco?"

"I tended Missus Taylor's gardens."

"With tobacco it's always something. Burning off seedbeds in the spring. Setting plants in the fields come May. Hoeing, topping, worming, suckering all summer. Cut and cure it in the fall. Strip and tie it in the winter and haul it to market."

"Yes, sir."

Luke says it this time in a smaller voice, and James knows he's afraid of all that James might ask of him. "Don't worry," he says. "You'll catch onto it. I suspect with Mrs. Taylor's gardens, it was always something."

"They were the most beautiful gardens in all of Maysville."

"I suspect they were," says James and drives on up the road, imagining the pride Luke took in those gardens and how odd he must feel now that he's gone from them. James thinks of John and how strange those first days were after he was born. James couldn't get over the mere fact of him. A boy. *His* boy. He could see the Martin ears on him, already too big for his wee head, and the cleft in his chin that quivered when he cried. James held him with hands that were then strong and nimble, not crippled with the years of work as they were now. He rocked the slight weight of him – no more than a farrow pig – and felt him squirm and twist. "You think you're a slippery one, don't you?" James said. "Well, I've got you. Don't think I don't. I've got you and you can't wiggle away."

But that's what he's done, James thinks – slipped away from him. All these years John's been leaving him a bit at a time, thinking he knows the way a man should live his life. And maybe John's been right, at least about this slave business. It pains James to admit it, but, given the way he feels around Luke, he has to think that John knows something, knows that it takes more than desire to own someone. You have to give up your soul. You have to be dead inside. You can't own a man and be a man yourself.

Crossing the old buffalo trace, James feels a wheel begin to wobble. He pulls back on the reins, commanding the horse to stop. "Whoa, hold up there," he says. Then he climbs down from the wagon to see what's wrong with the wheel.

It's the right front one. He gets down on his knees in the mud and sees that the linchpin has sheared off and has nearly worked its way free from the axle. "Linchpin's about to go," he calls up to Luke. He grabs the rim of the wheel and gives it a shake. "Look at the play in it. We'll have to jury-rig a make-do." He stands up, feeling the ache in his knees. "Come on down here," he says.

Luke swings his long legs over the side of the wagon and hops down with an ease that James envies.

"We need a sapling branch." James reaches under the buckboard's seat and draws out a hatchet. "Go up in the brush yonder and cut one. Hickory or walnut if you can find one quick enough."

He holds the hatchet out so Luke can take it. The blade, honed just that morning, gleams in the sunlight. Luke reaches out his hand and then stops, holds it frozen in midair. James looks him in the eyes and sees the uncertainty there. Or is it fear? Perhaps he's afraid to take the hatchet because he can't trust himself with it. Maybe, once he feels its weight, tests its sharp blade, he'll be tempted to split James's head open, take off north to Ohio. For a moment James thinks he's made a mistake, that he should go into the brush himself and cut the sapling branch, but at the same time, he understands that his gesture and whatever happens beyond it will have everything to do with the way he and Luke will get on for some time to come. He says it again: "Take it, Luke."

And Luke does. "A hickory, sir," he says.

"Or a walnut," James reminds him.

"Yes, sir," he says, and then he marches off toward the brush.

He's chopping away at a hickory sapling when the white boy comes crashing through the brush – a white boy with a crazy look in his eyes and the same jug ears as Mister James.

Luke straightens and lets his arm go down. He holds the hatchet at his side, its weight more than he can bear to lift. The white boy's face is cut, and his shirt sleeve is torn. He looks like he's on the run from someone, and, if that's the case, Luke doesn't want a thing to do with him or his trouble.

A turkey buzzard circles overhead, and Luke watches its shadow wheel past, dappling the brilliant green leaves of the hickory and the oak and the locust, momentarily softening the face of the white boy as it sweeps over him. Still, he frightens Luke. The stark mad look on his face suggests that he's caught between two fires, not knowing which way to jump, and might, at any moment, boil up and lash out at someone. And here's Luke, right smack-dab in his way.

The boy comes to him, picks his way through the brush until he's so close Luke can see his eyelids quiver. "That hatchet," he says. "How'd you come by it?"

Luke feels his hand tremble; the blade of the hatchet knocks against his leg. "Mister James gave it to me. He said, 'Go up yonder there and cut me a branch from a hickory sapling.'"

"James Martin?"

"Yes, sir. Mister James. He needs a linchpin for the wagon wheel. He says the other one's about to go. He's waiting for me down on the road."

A noise comes from the brush, and the white boy spins around as if someone has tapped him on the shoulder.

It's only blue jays thrashing around in the honeysuckle. The boy turns back to face Luke. "Do you know how to carve out a linchpin?"

Luke wonders what the proper answer might be. If he lies and says he does, the white boy might think him uppity. If he says no, he doesn't hardly think so, he's afraid the boy will call him worthless.

So he says nothing. He lowers his head and keeps his eyes on the ground, wishing that the boy would leave him be and let him go back to his chopping, a chore he can do just fine by himself, please and thank you.

But the boy's hand is on his now, the hand that holds the hatchet, and Luke feels a chill creep up the back of his neck. The boy's hand slips down to the hatchet's handle and tries to take it. Luke tightens his grip.

"It's all right," the boy says.

And Luke knows he has three choices: he can keep the hatchet and use it on the boy if need be; he can let it go, let the boy have it, and prepare himself for whatever is going to happen next; or they can stand there the way they are now, the two of them gripping the hatchet. Then Luke hears the brush crackle again, looks up, and thanks Jesus because he sees Mister James, the man who owns him now, come up from the road to see what's taking so long.

John turns and sees his father, and the first thing he notices is how give out he seems, how old. James braces himself by grabbing onto a branch. Then he pulls himself on up the hill to where John and Luke still hold the hatchet between them.

The turkey buzzard still circles overhead, and John thinks something must be dead nearby or about to die, anyway, the buzzard biding his time.

"I looked all over for you," James says, and at first John isn't sure whether he's talking to him with such yearning, such regret, or to the Negro who, John couldn't help but notice, looked at his father, when he first came through the brush, with thanksgiving. John was surprised to feel a pang of jealousy rise up in him. James says, "This morning. Before I lit out for town. I looked for you."

There are things they want to say to each other but can't manage in the company of Luke. John understands that this will always be the case. He won't be able to tell his father that he was right, that the trouble between them was never about this Negro who stands with them now, but about Elizabeth and the pious Gaunces, and now it's turned out that she doesn't care a snap about the fact that James Martin owns a slave. John wants to tell him about the evening he saw Mr. Hawkins bury Hannah, the way he did it without uttering a sound. Would it be that way, John wants to ask his father, if he would happen to die of the cholera? Would his father lay him to rest without a cry or a wail?

"You look like you been through it," James says. He reaches up and touches his fingers to the gash on John's cheek. "We'll have to get home and see to that." He lets his fingers linger, touching John gently. "We don't want that to fester."

"I hear you need a linchpin," John says.

James looks away from John and shakes his head. "Goddarn linchpin," he says in a small voice that tells John he's ashamed, not because the wagon wheel has broken down, but because he has gone to the slave auction and come away with this boy. John senses that, if his father could – if it were just the two of them standing there in the brush – he might tell him all of this. But right now he has a wagon wheel to repair.

"Better let the boy get on with his chopping," James says.

John feels his hand start to draw away from the hatchet handle, and he knows, as he does this, that he's agreeing to the Negro's presence in their family, to their ownership. And for the first time the shame of this truly touches him. He knows how much of a coward he is, afraid to go off into the world on his own, to be no party to this slaveholding.

"I'll carve out the linchpin for you," he says. Already he can feel the motion, his knife whittling down the wood, making it just the right size to fit through the axle and to stay there, at least long enough for the wagon to carry the three of them home.

One day, not long after the fisherman had drowned in Mack Jent's pond, my mother accepted a teaching position in the northern part of the state, and just like that, we were moving. My father sold our livestock. Trucks rumbled up our lane and took away our cattle and hogs. Suddenly the pens and pastures were empty.

We were moving because my mother had lost her job teaching grade school, and my father was willing to move three hundred miles north to a suburb of Chicago in exchange for the extra income the new teaching position would bring. He leased our farm to Mack Jent and became an absentee landlord.

It gave me an odd feeling to think of Mack Jent farming our

ground because I knew that my father didn't completely approve of his way of doing things. He planted too close to the fence lines, my father said. More than once he complained that Mack had planted over our property line. And he didn't keep his beans cultivated, or his machinery in tiptop shape. And he cut his wheat when it was still damp with dew, and on and on.

He had also brought a lawsuit against another farmer whose pick-up truck had come up too fast behind Mack's tractor on the County Line Road and rear-ended him. It hadn't been a serious accident, but Mack had claimed whiplash and back injuries and had won a settlement.

It was practically unheard of in those days for one member of our rural community to sue another member. It was considered bad form – unneighborly and unchristian. Good neighbors would find a way to work out their differences without involving the courts.

So Mack Jent had the reputation of someone not to be trusted. Why my father handed over our farm to him, even allowing him the use of our machinery, I still don't know, unless it was merely because the arrangement was convenient. Time was short, and someone had to be found. Mack was close and eager for the chance.

To me, he was like the Jents' terrier dog – tightly wound and tenacious, full of growl and snap. He wasn't ill-tempered or abusive the way my father often was; he was dangerous for a different reason. He was a wiseacre. When he joked with me, his barbs often stung. He teased me about being afraid of their dog, or having to double with Katrina when we rode Lightning. Maybe I ought to try riding side-saddle, he suggested. I know his teasing was meant to be good-natured, but I was a sensitive boy, one who suspected, even then, that I would never be the sort of man he was – gung-ho and brazen, unwilling to calculate risk and consequences.

He worked for Marathon Oil and did his farming at night and on the weekends. Everything about him said that he was ready to go, man, go. He wore overalls with nothing beneath them but bare skin and boxer shorts. He kept his hair in a sharp-bristled flattop. A Winston cigarette jounced from his lower lip as he gabbed. He must have talked his way into leasing our farm, the way he would eventually try to convince my father to sell him the whole kit and caboodle. By this time my father had come to regret the fact that he had ever allowed

Mack to sink a plowshare into our eighty acres. From time to time he would say, "I don't ever want this place sold to Mack Jent, or to any of his heirs." He had never accepted Mack's farming methods, and once, while Mack was our tenant, our International H tractor had burned to ruin.

"You see what you get," my father said, "when you're careless."

I never stopped, then, to consider the irony of his statement. What right did he have to accuse Mack when he himself had been careless with the corn picker and had ended up losing his hands? I only thought of the afternoon in the Jents' basement, when I had gone off half-cocked and wrestled Dan until he fell and hit his head. I had been reckless. I had thought I was defending Katrina and had ended up making her angry. Although we eventually put the incident behind us, the way children do, it seemed to mark the end of the way we had always known each other. Suddenly we were just two kids who went to the same school and happened to live near each other. There was nothing special between us. We may have even begun to pick up on the subtle tensions that smoldered between our fathers. We were moving in different directions. Then I was gone to Chicago, and though I saw Katrina in the summers, when we came back to our farm, we were never the same. When we were around each other, there was, at least for me, the feeling that I was a stranger, had perhaps always been one, allowed a momentary place in this world only through Katrina's deliberate kindness. I had ruined that; I would know it forever.

Elizabeth is there when the wagon comes up the hollow, and her heart leaps when she sees John sitting on the spring bench, the harness reins in his upturned hands. She sees the cut on his face and wonders what trouble he's found. She blames herself for the way he left her earlier. If she had only given herself to his passion – if she had said, "Yes, John. Oh, yes. I'll go with you. Wherever you say" – instead of trying to calm him with logic. Ever since he ran from the smokehouse, she's imagined him gone from her forever.

But now here he is, returned. She wants to run to him, throw herself into his arms and never let go. But his father is sitting beside him, his back humped up, and riding behind him is a Negro boy. He sits with his back to them. Elizabeth can see the tight weave of his hair, the brilliant sheen of his neck, glossy like the flank of a well-curried horse. She knows that James Martin now owns him, and this knowledge makes her think of the stories her father has told of the way the French invaded the Rhineland, burned the homes of the Palatines, drove them out into the open fields to sleep huddled on the cold ground, everything they owned lost to them forever. Never, her father has said, as long as he has anything to say about it, will a Gaunce hold slaves. "Let that sin be on someone else's soul," he says. "Not mine."

And now sin has come to settle on James Martin. Elizabeth wonders how the two families will ever survive the rift that she fears is coming. How will she ever be able to explain that John was never in favor of what his father meant to do without admitting – it comes rising in her without warning, this feeling she can no longer suppress; it seeps into her like an illness, like cholera, and she knows there's no cure – without admitting that she loves John Martin, that she's willing to do whatever it takes to be with him for life? She knew it that day when they were kids, when Prudence called him a mule, and Moses and Zed teased him, and John and Elizabeth ran off into the woods. She knew that she could never bear to be without him.

Now he moves past her, not even looking in her direction, as he drives the wagon to the barn. She can hear his father's voice, saying something about a wheel and a linchpin, and the Negro boy's soft murmur. "Yes, sir. Yes, sir." She can hear the harness buckles jangle as they come undone, and she feels herself slipping out of her old life. She's willing to risk her family for John. She wonders what Hannah Hawkins felt just before she died. Was it an airy feeling, a lifting, as if she were flying away?

Finally John comes up from the barn. They stand together under an oak tree while a squirrel chatters above them. The sky has turned a glorious blue, with just a few puffy white clouds floating high above the ridge.

"Your face," she says and raises her hand, meaning to touch his cheek.

He takes her hand in his own. "I want us to get married." He says this calmly, as if it's already a fact. "There's no law against it. We'll get married, and then we'll go away from here. Ohio or Pennsylvania, wherever seems right."

Elizabeth folds her fingers over his. She lays her head against his chest. She listens to his heart beating. She whispers in time with its rhythm. "Yes," she tells him. "Yes . . . yes . . . yes."

It happens quickly. By evening John lies in bed, sick in his stomach. He has no way of knowing – none of them do – that the cholera isn't in the air, as so many people believe. The bacteria are in the water that they drink, in the catfish they catch in the river. The bacterium *vibrio cholera* infects the small intestine, releasing a toxin that causes increased secretion of water and chloride ions. The result is a watery diarrhea. Death occurs because of severe dehydration.

"It's no wonder," Elizabeth tells James Martin. "He was out half the night in the rain."

"Over me," James says softly. He and Elizabeth are standing in the doorway, trying to stay out of the way of John's mother, who tends to him, fetching the chamber pot when he needs it, asking John's brother to empty it outside in the privy. "Over what I done," James says. "That Negro boy? Is that it?"

Elizabeth's pleasure in laying the blame on James startles her. "John wanted me to run off with him," she says. "He wanted to get away from you. Only I wouldn't go."

"So I done it. That's what you're saying. I'm the one who made this happen."

"I'd go now," says Elizabeth, tears filling her eyes. "I'd go with him in a heartbeat." She wipes at her eyes with the backs of her hands. "Kentucky," she says, and her voice is hoarse and ugly with venom.

She doesn't know that in her home, a home she would give up without a second thought if only John could be well, her father and the Reverend Michael Geoghegan have been talking about the slave question. They're sitting at the table, from which Sarah Gaunce has just cleared the supper dishes. Michael Geoghegan is trying to keep his voice low so as not to disturb Sarah, who is heating water at the fireplace. There are members of the Saltwell Methodist Church, he tells George Gaunce, who want to split off and form a proslavery "South" congregation. "And now," Michael Geoghegan says, "James Martin has seen fit to purchase a slave."

"James?" George says. "My Sarah's brother?"

"The very one." Michael Geoghegan frowns. His shaggy eyebrows knit together. "I saw it myself this morning when I had business in Carlisle. James Martin counting out his money at the auction block."

"I can hardly picture it."

"And what's more . . . well, perhaps I shouldn't say this." Michael Geoghegan twists his finger around in the long hairs of his mutton-chop. "But I honestly believe it's my duty. It appears that your Elizabeth and John Martin are sweet on each other."

"Is that something you know for a fact?"

"Poor Mr. Hawkins? The one who's lost three children to the cholera? He says he's seen Elizabeth and John holding hands up on the ridge in the clearing that overlooks the river."

"They're of an age," says George.

"Aye, but given the circumstances . . ."

George interrupts Michael Geoghegan to call to Sarah. "Sarah, have you seen Elizabeth? Where's she run off to tonight?"

"I imagine she's over to James's," Sarah says.

"As I was saying." Michael Geoghegan continues. "Given the fact that your brother-in-law has seen fit to become a slaveholder . . ."

But George isn't listening. He's thinking of Mr. Hawkins and how it must have torn at him to see Elizabeth and John, young and lovely up on the ridge, when three of his children lay dead. George listens to his three – Pru, and Moses, and Zed – running about outside, chasing a guinea hen. He doesn't know that they will all have long lives. In this time of cholera only a fool dares dream of the future. All he knows is that he wants Elizabeth here with him, not across the hollow at James's place, where a man is now enslaved.

"You're saying you wouldn't advise it," George says to Michael Geoghegan. "Then I expect we ought to go on over there."

Out at the barn Luke does as Mister James says. He scrapes back the cinders in the blacksmith's forge and hauls the slack to the ashpit. A shovel of hot ashes that Mister James has toted out from the kitchen fire lies smoldering on the forge.

"Now take some of these wood shavings here." Mister James scoops his hand into a pony keg and shows Luke the scrolled shavings. "And put them on that nozzle there. That's what we call the tuyere. Some folks say it 'tweer' or 'tue iron.' It's all the same. It's where the bellows blow out air."

Mister James, since coming to the barn, has spoken in a soft, kind voice, explaining to Luke with great patience how they'll forge a new linchpin for the wagon wheel. Luke listens to Mister James, remembering how Missus Taylor first taught him to care for her roses – to doctor them for aphids and thrips, to ward off blackspot, to prune them back after the killing frost. He remembers the ABCs book, its linen pages as soft and as floppy as rabbit ears in his hands. At first he had been afraid to touch the book, but Missus Taylor had said, "Go on. Open it up. You can't learn to read it if you don't open it." Inside had been pages divided into blocks, each with a bright red letter over a drawing – G, for example, with a goat, a gun, and a grindstone in its shadow. And there were lessons that taught words and sentences. Missus Taylor showed him how each letter had a sound, how the sounds combined to make words. *He is up.* Or, *We go in.* Or, *Let us go and see the goats.* He hears her voice now, reading along with his, the two of them chanting in the still, summer evening, their heads close together in the glow from the oil lamp. How she had suffered with the cholera. How he had wished her daughter would let him do what he could to save her.

Now the wood shavings are light and dry in his hands, and for a good while all he can do is hold them, recalling rose petals, the reader's linen pages, all things that have loved him with their touch. He can't bear to let the shavings go.

"What's the matter with you?" Mister James says, and now his voice is sharp. Luke is ashamed of himself for disappointing him. "Are you a crackbrain?" Mister James says. "Did I buy a crackbrain or someone with a penny's worth of sense?"

Luke knows something is wrong up at the house. He's heard Mister James's son, the one they call John, crying out in pain, and he's seen the other boy, John's brother, toting the chamber pot out to the privy. Mister James has shuffled about the barn, weary, as if he were wearing leg irons.

"Lay a pile on the nozzle," he says. He guides Luke's hand toward the tuyere. Suddenly he's kind again, patient. "There, that's it. Now we're stepping high."

He lifts the shovel of hot ashes and lays some over the shavings. He puts his face close and blows on the ashes. Soon the shavings are on fire.

"You see how I did it?" he says.

"Yes, sir."

"Now we got to rake the cinders back over those shavings and get to work with the bellows."

Mister James shows Luke the leather bellows and sets him to work pumping the lever that inflates them and then forces air out the tuyere into the forge.

"You just keep at that awhile," Mister James says. "That's right. Nice and easy. Let them fill and empty. Fill and empty. Pretty soon we'll have us a hot fire."

Luke is at his work when two white men come into the barn. One of them is stout, with whiskers on his face. He wears a hammertail coat and wipes his sweaty jowls with a white handkerchief. Mister James calls him Reverend.

"Reverend," he says. "It's about to get even hotter in here."

The other man is tall and thin with a gaunt face.

"I've brought George Gaunce with me," the Reverend says. "We're looking for Elizabeth."

"James," Mr. Gaunce says. "I never would have thought it of you. Our folks go back some time. As far as I know, no Martin ever owned another man."

Luke keeps his eyes on the bellows, expanding and deflating. He knows that the men have come to take issue with Mister James over Luke himself, over the fact that they are now master and slave. Luke fears that the Reverend and the other man, this George Gaunce, will somehow force Mister James to give him up. And then he might end up sold down the river, be worked to death in the cotton fields of Mississippi or the cane fields of Louisiana. At least here, from what he's gathered so far, no one is intent on driving him until he drops. He's heard about some slaves in Kentucky, fortunate enough to be rented out as apprentices to shoemakers, cabinetmakers, black-smiths, to be freed eventually, knowing a trade they can use to sup-port themselves. He's seen these men and their "freedom papers." Maybe, he thinks, his time with Mister James might lead to some-thing just like that.

"George and I have talked this over," the Reverend says, "and we've decided it would be wise if we kept Elizabeth and John away from each other."

"John's sick," Mister James says, and Luke hears the pain in his voice and something else, too – guilt. "He come down with a sick stomach before supper."

"Is it the cholera?" Mr. Gaunce asks.

"I don't rightly know," says Mister James. And then: "It could be. I expect so."

"Haven't you sent for the doctor?" the Reverend says.

With the steady whoosh of the bellows in his ears, Mister James's voice sounds far away to Luke. "I can't pay no doctor. I ain't got the money." Four hundred dollars, Luke thinks. The sum Mister James paid for him that morning.

At that moment the fire catches; tongues of flame lick up from the cinders. "Mister James, sir." Luke steps out from behind the forge. He can still feel the gentle rise and fall of the bellows in his arm. "I can heal him, sir." The men look at him with open mouths. "Your son, sir. I can lay hands to him. I can make him well."

This is the secret he has carried with him to the auction block, the fact that he is a healer. His very touch can draw out sickness. He knows the places on the body to press, to stroke, to knead. He can manipulate the humors, the fluids that ebb and flow. He can adjust an ailing constitution. He could have saved Missus Taylor – he's sure of it – had he only had the chance to lay hands to her. Her daughter wouldn't hear of it. She sent for the doctor. By nightfall Missus Taylor was dead.

Luke wants to heal this boy, this John, because he can see how dear he is to Mister James. As much as they hem and haw around it, the fact of the matter is clear. Luke saw it when he watched John whittle the sapling branch down to size, carve it into a linchpin while Mister James cooed to him: "That's right, honey. That's how you do it. You're almost there." Luke has no recollection of his own father, or his mother either. He only remembers Missus Taylor. He was always her boy. He knows how he felt when she died – like the earth had dropped away from him, like he was falling and falling. He doesn't want Mister James to know that feeling – that sinking, dizzy feeling that comes into a body and can't be purged, not even if someone, a healer, knows exactly where to press.

In the house Luke leans over the bed and lays his hands on John's stomach. The skin is cold and dry. Daylight's gone now, and Missus

Martin has moved a candle to the table beside the bed. She stands with Mister James in the shadows, her hands balled up in her apron. Mister James lays his gnarled hand on her shoulder and pets her the best he can.

The Reverend and Mr. Gaunce linger in the doorway. The blond-headed girl, the one they call Elizabeth, stands behind Luke, so close he can hear her short, panting breaths, as if her throat's closed off and she can hardly draw air. Her father has pleaded with her to come away, to stand with him out of the poisoned air around the sickbed, but she has refused to move. "John," she whispers from time to time. "John."

John's eyes are glassed over; his fingernails have a bluish tint. He stares up at the roof beams, unaware, it seems, that from time to time, his legs jerk and twitch, their muscles cramping.

"Someone ought to rub his legs, sir," Luke says to Mister James. "Rub out the knots."

Mister James lifts his hand from Missus Martin's shoulder and looks at it. Luke can see that he's trying to uncurl his fingers, that he wants, more than anything, to be able to touch his son and give him ease. But he can't, crippled up as he is, and Missus Martin won't take her hands out of the ball she's made with her apron. She looks across the bed, beyond Luke, and then bows her head.

Suddenly the girl, Elizabeth, is kneeling at the bed. She slips her hands under the hem of John's nightshirt, to rub the muscles in his calves. Luke understands that Missus Martin has passed her son over to the girl, that Elizabeth has acknowledged something by stepping forward.

"I would advise against touching him," the Reverend says.

"Elizabeth," says Mr. Gaunce. "For the love of God. Come away from there."

But she doesn't. She kneads the muscles of John's legs, and they begin to relax. Luke presses into the abdomen, runs a hand beneath John to the small of his back. He touches and touches and touches, and as he does, he begins to cry. He imagines he is saving Missus Taylor, bringing her back, saving himself.

John hears noises in his head: a crash of thunder, a roar of water rushing, a howl of wind. He feels the sting of sleet, the pelt of hail, the burn of hot iron lifted with bare hands from his father's forge. He's crying, but no tears come from his eyes. His shoulders heave; his arms flail. Then he feels a weight press down on him. He imagines a millstone dropped onto his chest. He thinks of Hannah Hawkins stretched out in her grave, her face turned up to the sky, dirt raining down from her father's shovel. He thinks of Elizabeth, of how she kissed him while they stood on the ridge above the riverbank. How sweet her taste; how sweet her kiss. He had wanted it to go on and on.

The noises shift and collide in his head. The clang of his father's hammer on the anvil, the gentle whirr of a flax wheel spinning, the squeal and creak of wagon wheels, a whisper from Elizabeth: "John. Oh, John." He wants to go toward that whisper, but he can't move. There's still the weight upon him, the pressure on his stomach and chest and back.

Then the sounds become more distinct, easier to bear, and every one of them makes him think, *Elizabeth.* The jingle of sleigh bells; the whisk and glide of dance steps on a plank floor; the flutter of quail, wings lifting them to flight. He hears a woman singing, a lilting voice rising and falling, softly calling to him. She's singing "The Girl I Left Behind Me."

O ne'er shall I forget the night,
The stars were bright above me
And gently lent their silv'ry light
When first she vowed to love me.

He strains to hear her, but her voice grows fainter and fainter, as if she's run far ahead. Light begins to fill him. It's like the first light of morning, a glimmer in the east. It's like the glitter of clear creek water running swiftly over stones; the sheen of white-barked sycamores along the river; the brilliant glare of midday, sun full up, the world bright and humming.

Then, suddenly, he's in a quiet place. The noises in his head are gone. He feels a pleasant heat in his hand, feels the pulsing of blood through a vein. He hears voices.

"He seems to be resting, Mother."

"That's all I can do, sir. Yes, sir, Mister James. That's all Luke can do right now."

"Gott bleibt bei diesem haus."

"What's that? Say it in proper English, George Gaunce."

"God abides in this house."

"Aye. Praise be to God."

John knows he's come back to the world, and at first he's not sure that's a good thing. He remembers the difficulty with his father. How will they ever know each other? Then John feels a weight rise from the bed. He opens his eyes, and there she is, leaning over him – Elizabeth. He speaks her name.

The last time I saw Katrina Jent was in 1988, at my mother's funeral. It was January, and southern Illinois was in the midst of a bitter cold spell. The temperature had dropped into the teens. The wind howled. Dusty ribbons of snow snaked across the streets. I imagined the wind moaning in the stovepipes of our deserted farmhouse.

My father had died six years earlier. We had made our peace. Through the grace of my mother's faith in goodness, we had managed to get beyond the anger that had raged between us for years. My mother – who had always been loving and kind, who had believed in God and redemption – had been slipping away from us a little at a time over the past three years. Small strokes – sometimes no more than a tingle in her lip, a loss of balance – had been destroying brain cells until, finally, she lay, aphasic, in a nursing home. I lived far away from her at the time, and on my visits – usually two or three times a year – I was always shaken by how much her condition had worsened. She had stood by, silent, while my father had whipped me, while in my teen years our anger had spurred physical confrontations. She had always seemed so helpless in my father's house. All she could do was endure and trust to God. Eventually the thousands of prayers that she must have said saved us. But I could do nothing to save her from the strokes that were taking her away.

I knew little of Katrina's own journey from childhood, only that she had married young, as soon as she had graduated from high school, that her mother had died from cancer soon after, that Katrina had worked for a time in a sheltered-care facility for mentally and physically challenged youths. I knew those facts, but they told me nothing of what she carried inside her – what private pains, demons, joys, fears. Once I had felt as close to her as I would have to a sister, but I couldn't see, then, the span of our adult lives, stretching out ahead of us like the long shadows our child bodies made when we were at play in the late-afternoon sunlight. I didn't know the different directions a life could take, how far someone could spin away from home, from themselves, from the people they swore they knew and loved.

"Lee."

I heard my name and turned, and there she was. Although over twenty-five years had passed since the days when she came for me and escorted me across the fields to her house, I recognized her immediately. Her dark hair was flecked with gray, but her face was still the face I had cherished all those years ago, at a time in my life when I needed her bright eyes, her kind smile.

"Hello, Katrina," I said, and I felt something open inside me, a door back to the boy I had been, timid and afraid.

"You remember me," she said, and I was stunned to think that she had imagined I wouldn't.

She introduced me to her husband, a friendly man who seemed as if he would be at ease in whatever situation he might find himself. He wouldn't be afraid of barbed wire snagging him as he crawled through a fence, or bees stinging him, or terrier dogs nipping at his ankles. And, if trouble found him, he wouldn't go off half-cocked, wrestle someone to the floor, bang his foe's head on the cement.

Katrina told a story about the day I fell off Lightning. "Do you remember that?" she asked me. She was smiling, her eyes sparkling, and I could see that she was taking great pleasure in telling this story.

"No," I said, and it was true. I had absolutely no memory of the event she described.

"I boosted you up, and I told you to hold onto the reins. Before I could get on, Lightning took off at a gallop. He hadn't gone but a few feet when you fell off."

Her husband chuckled, the way he must have on the drive to the funeral home, when Katrina had surely told him the same story. "You don't remember that?" he asked.

"I really don't." I wasn't sure which would be more shameful: to acknowledge the event or to display a faulty memory of it. "Was I hurt?" I asked Katrina.

"No, you weren't hurt. You were just scared. Poor little guy."

At one time I would have given anything for her sympathy. Oddly enough, on the day of my mother's funeral, I wanted none of it. I wanted no reminder of the timid boy I had been, the one for whom she had felt sorry. Both of my parents were now dead. I was the last to survive our turmoil, our shame. I was on the verge of the rest of my adult life, and the last thing I needed was to be reminded of what a "poor little guy" I had been.

"You know where we live," Katrina said to me. "Out on the highway. That big, white house on King's Hill. Stop in and see us sometime."

"I will," I told her, but, of course, I never did.

John wakes to the sound of birdsong, the chickadees and cardinals and wrens finding throat at first light. It has been this way all his life, here in the hills and hollows of Kentucky, the birds coming alive from their night's roosts, signaling another day. And here, on this late-summer morning in 1833, a morning no one thought John would live to see, it is the same. Soon the roosters will crow, and deer will come out to feed. The mist will lift from the hollows, and the dew will dry on the bluegrass. John will sit up in bed and see Elizabeth, and his mother and father, and his brother, and Luke, all of them gathered in the log house, anxious for light so they can know the earth has turned around again and brought John with it.

"Well, you gave us a scare," his father says. "If it hadn't been for Luke . . ."

"Luke?" says John.

"That's right," says his mother. "He doctored you. He brought you around."

Luke has toted water from the cistern and is setting a kettle to boil on the hearth. He doesn't turn around at the mention of his name, preferring to leave the family to itself, to the things they have to say to one another.

"I'll give Luke his choice," James says. "To stay here with us or to go on as a freedman. Does that sound all right, John?"

"You spent money," John says. "You'd just let him go?"

"I got my money's worth. What he done for you? It was like nothing I ever seen. Don't you worry about that four hundred dollars. I'm glad I spent every cent of it. I don't know of nothing Luke could do that would make me feel any different."

Luke rakes ashes from the fire, lays on more wood. A freedman? His hands tremble with the thought of it. He likes thinking that no matter what he chooses, to go off on his own or to stay and work for Mister James, this family, in the years to come, down through generations and generations of ancestors, long after Luke himself is gone, will tell the story of the way he brought John Martin back from the dead.

"I'm thirsty," John says, and Luke brings a dipper of water to the bed.

"Let me hold it for you, Mister John." He brings the dipper to John's lips. "Sip it slow, now. Your belly won't stand too much too fast."

John lets Luke hold the dipper to his mouth, and as he drinks, he knows that this moment has nothing to do with a slave serving his master. It is simply a kindness one man pays to another.

There were times when I had to hold a Pepsi bottle so my father could drink from it. He came in from the fields, sweat-soaked and parched, and on occasion, when he tried to open his hook, the bands at its base snapped and rendered the pincers useless. "Hold that bottle up so I can get a swallow," he said, and I put the bottle to his lips and tipped it up. He closed his mouth around the neck, and, as he drank, his eyes got wide the way calves' did when they stretched out their necks to suck milk from a nippled bottle. He seemed so needy to me then. I forgave every time he had whipped me. He drank like a man who had wandered too long in a desert. He was thirsty, and I was the one he needed to give him aid.

In my teen years, in answer to my mother's prayers, we joined the church – first I, and then my father. We confessed our sins, we were baptized, we rose up from the water into our new lives. Sometimes during communion services, I held a thimble-sized glass of grape juice to his lips so he could drink. He touched the tip of his hook to my hand, and together we lifted the dainty glass. I was always afraid that we would bobble it, that it would fall to the floor and shatter, but it never did. It survived our handling as we had both weathered our rough strife.

*

James Martin rises from the rocking chair where he dozed off toward dawn. Most of the night he watched John sleep, took in the steady rise and fall of his chest the way he once did when John was a baby asleep in his cradle. And now here he is, sitting up, sipping water from the dipper. James looks at Luke, at the way his lips part and his chin rises, as if he himself were drinking. And James realizes that his own mouth is open. He sees that his wife is doing the same thing. Elizabeth, who sits on a chair by the bed – she, too, is leaning forward, her mouth open.

I try to imagine the first Martins who crossed the Atlantic and finally set foot on dry land. Did they fall down on their knees, give thanks for safe passage? Did they hold babies in their arms, whisper promises to them of the good life to come?

On October 24, 1833, after harvest is done, Elizabeth Gaunce and John A. Martin will marry. The Reverend Michael Geoghegan will perform the service. One night a few weeks later, a meteor shower lights the sky. The heavens blaze. John wakes to the light, to the sizzle of dry brush catching fire on the hills.

"Is the world ending?" he says to Elizabeth.

"Oh, no. It can't end now." She wants to fall back asleep beside him, to think they have years and years ahead of them. Already the first child, William, is taking life in her womb. "Don't say it, John. It couldn't be true."

They wrap their arms around each other and close their eyes. John trembles with the fear that the world is burning – burning all of them to ash – and what saddens him most is the thought that after the trouble with his father, after the cholera and Luke who saved him, there might be no one to know how each one of them, no matter their torment – no matter the anguish between them – had truly loved the earth, its early-morning rise of birdsong in the woodlands of Kentucky, where the stone tips of the first people's spears and lances still turn up from the soil, from the forest floor.

I hold one now in my hand, feel its serrated edges, its point, rub my thumb over the veins someone's careful honing raised from stone.

3
Earth Hunger

I don't know how my great-great-grandmother, Elizabeth Gaunce, died. No death record exists; no family member remains who might know. The only fact I have is this: her remains lie buried in a country graveyard in Christy Township in Illinois – Brian Cemetery, located just to the north of Lukin Township in the southwest quarter of section thirty. Her husband, John A. Martin, is buried a few miles to the south, in Lukin. This separation saddens me. This distance – Elizabeth so close and yet far enough removed to be forgotten. At no time, during the years I visited family graves with my parents on Decoration Day, do I recall making a trip to the Brian Cemetery. But all the while, as I rode the bus to the Lukin School, as my father drove the township roads, as winter's snows moved in, spring rains, summer heat, the grave was there, waiting so patiently, over 130 years, and now at last I've found it.

The Brian Cemetery is a flat piece of land atop a hill rimmed with hickory trees and creeper vines. Five stone steps, cut into the hillside, lead up from the gravel road to the graves. The oldest markers, along the western edge, have been overwhelmed with vines and moss. The black husks of hickory nuts, cracked open by squirrels, lie scattered on the ground. The day is warm and humid – late June in southern Illinois – but there in the shade of the hickories the temperature cools, the leaves rustle, their rattling the only sound, save the occasional call of a crow. Out across the field timothy grass waves and bends.

The Lawrence County cemetery book I've consulted indicates that Elizabeth Martin's grave is in row four, two plots to the south of that of her daughter Nancy A., who died in 1860. To my amazement the engraving on Nancy's stone is legible. Easily, I read the inscription, and I see that what I've suspected is true. The cemetery book indicates that Nancy was the daughter of J. *W.* and E. Martin. The stone clearly reads J. *A.* and E. Martin.

Elizabeth's stone has fallen, and slowly over the years it's sunk into the ground so only a portion is visible in the grass, a patch of white, the stone bleached by the years and years of sun, the sweep of wind. I kneel beside it and trace my fingers over its weathered face. I feel the remains of some long-ago etching, too worn and scarred now to ever be read, but I know that somewhere in the tangled tracks of dead-end grooves lies my great-great-grandmother's name, Elizabeth.

What did they call her? The people who loved her. Eliza? Lizzie? Beth? How did my great-great-grandfather tell her, long ago in Kentucky, that he thought they should pick up and go north?

Did he say, "Lizzie, I'm tired of these hills, worn to death prying up rocks before I can plow a furrow"?

Or was it, "I can't bear to live in a slave state. Up in Ohio everyone goes free"?

Perhaps it was the depression of 1837 that ran them out of Kentucky, or maybe it was merely "earth hunger," the urge to move on, the belief that there was always more land, better land, somewhere else.

They would have traveled overland with oxen and wagon, up the Maysville Road to the Ohio River. They would have crossed on flatboats – Elizabeth and John A., and their children William and Sarah – and then continued on, maybe thirty miles more, to Scott Township in Brown County, where other families from Nicholas County had already gone (the Cotrells, the Fites). One of the Fites, Reuben, had married John's sister Hethy.

John and Elizabeth would buy two acres on the waters of White Oak Creek. Such a humble plot of land, but to them, after all that had happened in Kentucky – John nearly dying of the cholera – it must have seemed like paradise.

On my father's farm, when I was a boy, I knew how to find the quiet, hidden places – the crevices of gullies, the deep beds of grain wagons, the hollowed-out spaces behind hay bales or in fence rows of honeysuckle. I liked to listen to my parents' voices when they didn't know I was nearby. It was as close as I could come to an idea of the people they had been before I happened along. Perhaps I felt guilty for disturbing their life together. Maybe I hid and eavesdropped as a kindness paid to them, a momentary relief from the burdens of parenting.

I was old enough to play without supervision, and I had the run of our eighty acres. There were no wild animals that might attack me, no uncovered wells to fall into, no kidnappers lurking. My parents could let me go and trust that I would return safely. And go I did, into hiding, delighted when I heard their private conversations, the words never meant for my ears.

Some mornings, before I got out of bed, I heard them talking in the kitchen. One morning my father said, "You'd think the world was ending. Just listen to that rain."

I could hear the rain driving hard against my bedroom window. Through the streaked glass I saw the sassafras saplings in the fence row bending over from the force of the wind. The rain pelted our roof, blew down our stovepipes, beat against the tin roof of the old smokehouse in our backyard. It was early spring, and the rain had been with us for days, the sky dark, the saturated earth dappled with puddles, the creeks rising and spilling over the township roads.

Soon, I knew, we would find baby rabbits drowned in the freshwater spring in our barnlot. I remember my father kneeling at the spring and clamping his hook around a rabbit's hind legs, pulling it, sleek and still, from the water, its eyes closed, the delicate tabs of its ears slicked back against its skull. I had seen my father birth calves when they were breech, kneeling in the straw of a stall to grab the hind legs and pull. I had watched him pick baby pigs up by their tails and move them out of the way of the sow so she wouldn't roll over and crush them. Runt pigs, the ones that would never make any money at market, he killed with the blow of a sledgehammer. Once, when a stray dog dropped a litter of pups under our smokehouse, my father, after trying to find homes for them, carried them in a cardboard box to the cement culvert at the end of our lane and killed them one by one by striking their heads against the stone. He came back crying.

"We couldn't afford to feed them," he said.

But I didn't know then, and still don't, how to feel sorry for him. He seemed brutal to me, savage beyond redemption.

Then, the morning it was raining, I heard him speak to my mother in a reverent voice, the sort of voice he must have used to woo her. "You don't think it could, do you? The world? End in a flood?"

My mother, a devout woman, said, "I don't expect it's our place to wonder about such things. It's just our job to keep living. Keep doing the best we can."

"God said the next time he destroyed the earth it'd be with fire."

I had never suspected that my father knew anything at all about the Bible. In those days he didn't go to church with my mother and me. He was a rough talker, a man of force. But that morning, when he talked about Noah and the ark, about God's promise to one day destroy the earth with fire, it was clear that at one time in his life he had known a religious faith and that it had mattered to him. He sounded as awe-struck and as shy as I was in Sunday School when I learned the story of Shadrach, Meshach, and Abednego, cast into the furnace.

"Oh, but listen to that rain," my father said. "Golly."

John Martin was a Methodist, which means he would have believed that grace was readily available to anyone who might choose to accept it. I imagine him turning his eyes toward Ohio, only twenty-seven, so much of his life ahead of him. He must believe in new beginnings, even for his father, who bought the slave, Luke, and then set him free.

James, too, decides to pick up and move to Ohio, thereby forever separating my branch of the Martin family from the South. "There's not a good price for tobacco this year," he tells John. "And the corn? Might as well throw it to the hogs. If you want to be setting out, I'd be one step ahead of you."

And what of Elizabeth? She is the one to leave her father and mother behind in Kentucky. George Gaunce will die there, as will his wife, Sarah. Elizabeth will be far away from them, following John's wanderlust – first to Ohio, and then to Indiana, and finally to Illinois, where she will die on a late-October day in 1867 and come to rest atop the hill of the Brian Cemetery in the shade of the hickory trees, far from the hollows of Kentucky where she first drew breath, where now, as a friendly stranger in Carlisle told me when I visited last summer, "There's scads of Gaunces hereabouts."

That summer Kentucky was suffering through a drought. The bluegrass was parched and brown, and the rolling hills had the look of autumn. And, too, there was the odor of decay in the air – leaves withering and dropping from the trees, the dusty scent of the dry grass. Along the foothills patches of tobacco yellowed. If not for temperatures in the mid nineties it would have been easy, as I drove along the narrow road winding back into the hills toward Saltwell, the area where the Martins and the Gaunces had owned land, to have believed that it was the fall of the year, that harvest was almost on. I could imagine John Martin chopping tobacco, coming up from the patch in the bluish gray light that deepened now around me. A deer, the points of its rack silhouetted against the sky, appeared at the crest of a hill.

"There," I whispered to Deb, pointing to her right as I slowed the car. "A deer."

Before she could ready her camera and snap the shot, he was gone.

"Sorry," she said.

"It's all right," I told her.

And it was. Dark was falling, and I was quite content. A feeling came over me that I had only experienced the few times I had returned to my father's farm in Illinois after my parents' deaths – a feeling that I was somehow home, called back to the lands of my ancestors, where spirit and earth rejoined.

The next day at the public library in Carlisle, where I sat looking at census records, a woman said to me, "What family you trying to sort out?"

"Martin," I told her.

"You and a load of others," she said. She was a short woman in a lime green pantsuit. Her face, something about her chin and eyes, put me in mind of my great-aunt Lillie. This woman seemed familiar to me, an image of so many Martins and Inyarts and Ridgleys and Bells. "There was a Nehemiah Martin." She tipped back her head and peered at me through the round lenses of her glasses. "He married Drucilla Cottrell. He was the first constable of Nicholas County."

"My great-great-grandfather was John A. Martin." I felt like a small boy, lost, who believes that if he keeps saying his name, eventually strangers will take him in and somehow help him find his way home. "His wife was Elizabeth Gaunce."

"There's an old man in town, Boswell Keller. He's been trying to sort out the Martins for years. If he hasn't done it, I doubt it can be done. Folks like you're hunting, they didn't bring much when they came and didn't leave much when they took a notion to move on."

So often, in my research, I had looked with envy at the diaries and letters and wills other families had left.

"How would I find this Mr. Keller?" I hoped that he might know things I didn't.

"You going to be in town awhile?"

"Today," I said.

"I'll see to it."

"You'll arrange it? But how will you know how to find me?"

"It's a small town. Lord knows how many people watching you already, what with you driving that car with Texas plates."

The owner of the bed and breakfast where my wife and I were staying had told us about Mozart Hall, an old performance hall that was located above a variety store just off the square. The store held a little bit of everything: groceries, hardware, furniture, a completely operable Model T Ford. The store owner, a spry elderly man, switched on the Model T's headlights for us and sounded its "kahooga" horn.

"Folks get a kick out of that," he said. Then he led us upstairs and showed us where the stage had been and the spots on the ceiling where the oil-lamp chandeliers had hung from their chains. I imagined the smoke-laced air, heavy with the scent of coal oil, and the smells of the patrons, the wool of their clothing in winter – coats and shawls and dresses that had soaked up the aromas of hot cooking grease, sweat, wood-burning fires.

Along the walls were the remains of old playbills advertising performances of "The Brilliant Operatic Comedy," *In Old Madrid*, and "The Amazing Wind Dancers" in *Humpty Dumpty*.

"Some folks over in Lexington," the elderly store owner told us, "came out and peeled back the wallpaper to find the posters beneath it. Oh, they were real particular about it. I guess some folks are interested in such things."

I thought of the "folks from Lexington," their fingers trembling as they flecked away the paper, not sure what treasures they might find on the other side. I considered my own attempts to travel back through the generations of my father's family. What did I hope to find along the way? Why was it that others, like Deb, had little interest in their own family histories? Was it some lack in me, some dissatisfaction with the here and now, that sent me miles across the country to inspect old documents in county courthouses, to page through census records? Did I hope to discover my ancestors, or did I want their spirits to discover me?

Downstairs I paid the elderly gentleman for a bag of peaches, and when I turned around, the woman in the lime green pantsuit was standing behind me as if she were the shadow I cast. I hadn't heard her come into the store, hadn't heard the door open or the jingle of its bell, hadn't heard her footsteps on the floor or felt a tickle of air. It was as if she had suddenly materialized behind me.

"Boswell Keller," she said. "He's over to the cafe."

I would be forty-four that fall; Deb would soon be forty-two. In the winter we had decided to try to have a child, something we had always delayed as we moved about the country, trying to establish careers. And, too, Deb had always doubted that she wanted the experience of motherhood. She dreaded the physical challenges of pregnancy and delivery. Her own mother had been domineering and forbidding, and Deb feared she would become a similar woman, particularly if she happened to have a daughter.

I have to admit that I had my own doubts about being a parent. I feared that, like my father, I might be impatient and quick-tempered, and I wondered whether I was suited to deal with the daily dramas having a child would surely bring. Although I could very well imagine, and often longed for, the sound of our child's voice filling our home – dreamed of this person who would be a blend of Deb and me – I wondered whether I was too selfish to be a father. After all those years of having time and space to do what I wanted when I wanted, how would I make room for a baby and its needs and demands?

Deb and I were both afraid, but something that winter – it may have been time moving ahead, or perhaps the fact that we were at a place in our lives where we felt secure (we owned our house, had jobs that would last, a marriage that felt safe), or maybe just our living in Texas, so far from the few family members we had in Illinois – made us feel that it was time to start a family of our own. Maybe we were just afraid of being alone.

I still remember those days and how, when I went for my morning run and let my mind wander over how our lives might be about to change, I felt such thrill and fear; the possibility of being a father amazed and humbled me. It was too large and magnificent and terrifying.

Our attempts to get pregnant soon ended. I received a job offer in the Midwest, and we agreed it would be wise not to think about having a baby until we had decided what to do about the job offer. In the end, for financial reasons, we decided to stay in Texas, and when I suggested to Deb that we could now go ahead with our plans, she said she wasn't sure that getting pregnant was really what she wanted to do. It saddened me to hear this, but I was also relieved. Neither of us, it seemed, was sure enough; we both had too much that we feared. So that summer, in Carlisle, we both knew with a permanence that we had avoided for years that we would remain childless. Perhaps that was why I was chasing after ghosts, and why I found myself in the Carlisle Cafe, face to face with Boswell Keller.

He was tall and gaunt, a picture of what I will probably look like if I have the fortune to reach his advanced age. He had the same oversized ears I've inherited from the Martins, and the vertical worry lines in his brow from years of narrowing the eyes in concern. He wore brogans and khaki work pants that were either too short or seemed that way because he wore no socks. He had white shins and bony ankles. He was also hard of hearing.

"My name is Lee Martin," I shouted. By nature I'm soft-spoken, often shy and reserved. It was difficult for me, slightly embarrassing, to announce myself so loudly in the presence of curious strangers.

Boswell Keller cupped his hand around his ear. "Come again?" he said.

"Lee Martin." I forced myself to increase my volume even more. "I understand that you've been researching the Martins here in Nicholas County."

Where was the woman in the lime green pantsuit? I wished for someone to help me with this conversation, someone to do my shouting for me. Boswell Keller lowered his hand. He laid it flat on the table and spread his fingers. He leaned toward me, squinting.

"You a Martin?" he said.

"That's right."

"Come again?"

"Yes," I said, as loudly as I could.

The cafe was full of cigarette smoke that stung my eyes and settled in my throat and made it difficult for me to breathe. Had I not wanted information so badly, I never would have been in such a place.

"My great-grandmother was a Gaunce," Boswell Keller said. "Susannah."

Now, I thought, we're finally getting somewhere. "My great-great-grandmother was Susannah's sister, Elizabeth. She married John A. Martin. Have you ever heard of him?"

"No, but I know Susannah's mother was a Martin. Sarah."

"Who were her people?"

Boswell Keller raised his hand. He pointed his finger at me, let it hang there in the smoky air. Here it comes, I thought, the information I had yet to discover, the names of John A. Martin's parents. I was eager to step back one more generation. "Here's what I've studied out," Boswell Keller said. He folded in his finger and let his hand drop back to the table. "There was a world of Martins back then."

It would be later, after clues and hints, eliminations and deductions, that I would speculate that John A.'s father had been James, that he had been a brother to Sarah and Nehemiah. But on that day in the cafe I knew I had reached a dead end.

"I just can't get it all studied out," Boswell Keller said.

I heard the regret in his voice, and I knew that he had turned this over in his mind again and again. We were fellow travelers, obsessed with the past, but Boswell Keller was more desperate because he knew that his time was running out.

I reached across the table and shook his hand. "I guess we're some kind of cousins," I said.

"Yes, sir." He smiled and squeezed my hand. "I reckon we are."

That moment made it all worthwhile – the smoky air, the shouting I had done. I was glad that I had found Boswell Keller, thankful that I had made my journey to Kentucky, if for no other reason than to look into the face of this man and to see in his eyes how thankful he was that I had come.

*

In Brown County, Ohio, the land for the most part is flat – a limestone clay soil, striped with sandy loam. Fertile land for growing wheat, corn, and hay. After the rocky hills of Nicholas County, Kentucky, John Martin must be thankful for whatever small parcel of land he can own. In the White Oak Valley he finds a wealth of timber for building his house and for fuel come winter. There are black and white walnut trees, ash, elm, hickory, linn, sycamore, white oak, and beech. All summer the leaves stir and flash their paler green undersides when the wind blows through them. The sky above the flat land is always open and blue; the air, John swears, is easier to breathe.

"More room here," he says to Elizabeth. "Aren't you glad we come?"

"It's different from Kentucky. I'll grant you that."

"Feels like home, Lizzie. In here." He thumps his chest. "Where it counts. It feels like I'm home."

At times Elizabeth is as happy as she's ever been. She loves to watch her little Sarah, nearly three now, run after meadowlarks as they scurry along on their twiggy legs. "Birdie," Sarah calls. "Here, birdie. Tweet, tweet." William, a year older than Sarah, likes to stick his face into the delicate petals of tiger lilies, the trumpets of Virginia creeper vines, and breathe in their aromas. Sometimes he falls over in the tall grass and lies there as if he's drunk on the fragrance.

While John and his father are building homes, they and their families live with the Fites, Reuben and Hethy. What a houseful! Some of the children sleep in the barn. Reuben's younger brother, Jesephettis – the one they call Joseph – will be the schoolmaster at New Hope come fall, though he's barely nineteen. He has narrow, long-fingered hands that fascinate Elizabeth. So lovely they are – smooth-skinned and hairless, the nails pared and clean. She loves to sit by the fire of an evening and watch him read. She takes note of the way he licks his finger before he turns a page. She keeps her own hands, red and chapped from dishwater and lye soap, hidden under her apron. She imagines John's hands, nicked and scarred from times when ax blades and knives and hay sickles slipped, and his father's hands, clawed and crippled from years of farm work.

What a sort this Joseph is, this schoolmaster with the lovely hands. Night after night Elizabeth imagines what they would feel like if they were ever to touch her. Then, by the reason of daylight, she scolds herself. She works at her chores, eager to keep her mind from such wicked thoughts.

But then she skins her knuckles gritting corn or burns her fingers cooking at the fire, and right away she thinks of Joseph's beautiful hands, as smooth as corn silk, and she wishes that she had never left Kentucky, never opened the world so wide and found herself looking about, starved for the next extraordinary sight.

I've spent the better part of two days trying to recall the things I've seen that have truly amazed me – stopped me dead in my tracks and filled me with wonder and awe. The sort of moment Annie Dillard had at Tinker Creek when she saw a frog dissolve until nothing was left but a skin of green on the surface of the pond. Or the kind Tim O'Brien portrays in his novel *In the Lake of the Woods*: two snakes joined in a circle, each swallowing the tail end of the other, each working its way toward the other's head.

Next to these two examples, I have little to offer. You'd think, since I grew up on a farm, close to the earth and the seasons, to the natural world displaying its miracles, I'd have a storehouse of such moments. But I don't, and that fact disturbs me. Where have I been while the universe has been putting on its show? Perhaps I've spent too much time alone in rooms with books, reading about someone else's experiences.

Or maybe I'm not so different from most people. At dinner this evening I ask my friends what their moments have been. What have they seen? I want to know. What do they remember? Dolphins leaping and arcing off the coast of Mexico, the bright light of a satellite tracking across the New Hampshire sky, a sea turtle who needed help to dig away the sand so she could lay her eggs on a beach in Florida.

Late one afternoon, in the cusp between summer and fall, when the trees were still green but wouldn't be for long, I saw a sycamore turn golden for a moment. Something about the angle of the sun on the horizon, combined with the late season, cast an ethereal glow. At first it looked like the broad leaves had burst into flames and would burn to ash. Then, as the wind moved them, they shimmered and flashed and seemed to turn into liquid.

But no, that wasn't it at all. The light was more muted, the color of the leaves more amber – a stream of honey. It's so hard to say what I saw, and that's what stays with me – the mystery. Even now, in memory, I can't solve it. I don't even want to find out how it happened. I only want to recall that moment when the world seemed amazing to me. How lucky I was to part the curtains at just that moment and to see the sycamore tree transformed.

Still, it seems paltry given the number of years I've been around. Why should I thirst for more moments like this one? Perhaps I want the universe to validate me as a worthy receptor. Trust me, I want to say. Show me what you're reluctant to show someone else. Perhaps I want to be blessed.

Because my father was so often an angry man – because he and I both raised our voices and said ugly things to each other – in public I became a quiet boy. Early on, in photographs, my face tips down, my eyes shy before the camera. I'm waiting, it seems – waiting for some sign that it's all right for me to be alive. So often I tiptoe through my days, afraid that someone will take notice of me. It is the act of disappearing I learn in my father's house, where sometimes the slightest movement, the wrong word, can send him into a rage. He curses me, whips me, chases me as I run down our lane. I want to make him happy, to keep him from his anger. I want to be enough to leech the bitterness from him, the rage, the frustration he feels because he has no hands. I want to turn him golden.

And sometimes I do. Sometimes I charm him, and he speaks to me with tenderness, with the gentle voice he used with my mother the rainy morning when he wondered whether God would flood the earth. I reach my father most often through physical weakness, through the breakdown of the body, a language he understands. When my nose bleeds, as it does frequently in these days, he sometimes soaks a washcloth in warm water and tells me to tip back my head. "Don't cry, honey," he says. "It'll stop and you'll be as good as new."

He even ventures to touch me with the point of his hook, rubbing it as gently as he can over my head. Such moments are precious to me because they are too few. If I could find them every minute of every hour, I would. But most often I'm on guard, wary of my father's temper. I'm like the rabbit frozen in the brush, sniffing danger; the walkingstick clinging to a twig, the one nearly the same color, which will make it nearly impossible to spot him; the opossum that goes limp, pretends to be dead, and even if prodded or poked refuses to make a sound.

Through the years, because I've been quiet, people have sometimes thought me snobbish and rude. Others, the needy ones, have sought me out so they could tell me their secrets. Who would I ever tell? my confessors must have thought. After all, I was so quiet.

I imagine Elizabeth whispering to me now, and what she says is this: "My lands. You wouldn't believe how Joseph could make me feel – just the sight of his hands. Mercy. Sometimes I wished the crows would peck out my eyes."

And what I wish I could tell her is: It's all right. It's all love. It's just us being alive.

Because my early years were filled with the cold steel of my father's hooks, the lash of his belt, I have always been susceptible to physical beauty – not the stunning, fashion-model looks that seem to me manufactured, alien, inhuman, but the distinct, nicely formed feature that touches, with its perfection, the bruised spirit I still carry beneath my skin. The lips or collar bones or ankles that seem granted by a beneficent creator, a force that intends for us to be human to one another, to be loved by virtue of our common failing and want.

My father's eyes were blue with hazel flecks, and no matter how he hurt me, I never tired of looking at those eyes, which I imagine welling with tears the moment he knew his hands were lost to him forever. When I was young, he wore a bright red sport coat made from corduroy. I loved the feel of the fabric, loved it so much that I tried to wear the coat myself. I'm six in the photograph I have that shows me standing in our farmyard, dwarfed inside the coat's great bulk. Its hem falls below my knees. I've raised my right arm to shield my eyes from the sun, and my fingers are barely visible inside the sleeve. They don't look like fingers at all, but more like the sutured ends of my father's stumps. The left sleeve dangles, long and empty, at my side, as if I have nothing at all to fill it.

What is this emptiness? Elizabeth wonders. This hunger she feels inside her? Is it a yearning for her parents left behind in Kentucky? Is it a fear that John and his father won't finish the houses by winter and will leave them all cooped up and underfoot with the Fites? Or is it love – a love she can't even put a name to, only know by the sad, sweet ache that hollows her out each time she sees Joseph's darling hands?

It has been months since she and John have touched, other than an occasional brush of hands while taking or receiving little William or Sarah, or a tickle of skin while shifting about at night on the corn-shuck mattress. They sleep in a corner of the loft, near Reuben and Hethy, across from James and his wife. Elizabeth lies awake listening to the snores and the whistles of the men in the house, and the sweet murmurs of the children, dreaming. She wonders what the women dream: her mother-in-law and Hethy and John's sister Malinda. Do they dream of lives they can't say? Do they make secret journeys in the night and then wake, as she does, doubting that they know them-selves at all, wondering what's real: the lives they move through each day or the ones they escape to in their sleep?

More and more these days Elizabeth's dreams are filled with Jo-seph. He steals in without warning. She'll be dreaming of Sarah chas-ing meadowlarks, or William sniffing the flowers of creeper vines, and then, in a snap, the meadowlarks will lift up in flight and their wings will turn into Joseph's lovely hands, or she'll wade out through the creeper vines to fetch William, only to find Joseph waiting, reaching out to claim her.

And John, she thinks, suspects none of this. One evening they walk back into the woods to pick blackberries, and he puts his hand on her waist and pulls her to him for a kiss.

"God, Lizzie," he says. "I've missed you."

"Why, John Martin." She laughs. "I haven't been gone anywhere."

"I've missed us." She feels him growing hard against her thigh. "Missed our hootie-tootie time. Can't get much of that what with the houseful we've got."

That's what he's always called their lovemaking – "hootie-tootie." Sometimes he says it when he's inside her, moving fast. "Hootie, hootie, hootie." How funny it is to her, and how sweet – the joy of it, the sheer and utter joy. She realizes she's missed that, too, the months they've been with the Fites, and she imagines the emptiness she feels is only that lack, that she has become enchanted with Joseph's hands because she and John have been robbed of their intimacy.

Now she lets him lay her down and raise the skirt of her dress. She smells the rotting leaves around her, rotting since last fall, when they tumbled down from the white oaks and the hickory trees. She feels them, soft and damp beneath her.

John is unbuttoning his trousers. "John," she says, "we're wicked."

But she doesn't say it in earnest. She doesn't stop him, not even when she senses a movement off to her left, when she sees the light change ever so slightly, when she knows someone is hidden in the undergrowth, watching them.

Back at the house everyone makes a fuss over the buckets of berries – so juicy, so sweet. Elizabeth bends over to pick up Sarah, and William plucks a twig from her hair.

"Mama," he says, "did you fall?"

Elizabeth's hands fly to her head, her neck, her shoulders, her fingers feeling for stray bits of leaves.

"Here, let me," Joseph says. Then his hands are on her, his beautiful hands, brushing across her back, her arms.

"Yes," she says to William. "Mama fell."

She knows she should be embarrassed; it's no secret now what she and John have been up to in the woods. But all she can think of is how close Joseph is to her. She smells the must of the forest on him, that and the fresh scent of cedar, and she knows he was the one, hidden away, watching.

When I was a child, my mother told me that God was watching over us, that he saw everything we did.

"Everything?" I said.

"Yes," she told me. "Everything."

"Does God love me?"

"Very much."

"Do you love me?"

"Of course I do, you silly."

"And Daddy?"

"Yes, Daddy loves you, too."

He whipped me with his belt, the yardstick, a switch cut from a persimmon sapling. In some ways we were too much alike – both of us stubborn, quick to anger – and in other ways we were very different. He was boisterous and outgoing; I was shy and withdrawn. But I was also quick to challenge him, to return the spunk he had taught me, and when we butted heads, there was no sign of love between us. There were only shouts and threats and curses and the lash of the yardstick or the switch or the belt.

And my mother couldn't stop this, nor my father, nor I – none of us, no matter how much we believed in God.

Early one morning Elizabeth and Malinda are outside scrubbing clothes when Joseph comes up the lane, a palm-leaf hat on his head, his sleeves rolled to his elbows.

"Ladies." He tips his hat toward Elizabeth and Malinda. "You're a divine sight this morning. As welcome as the flowers in May. Very blissful."

"Blissful." Malinda says this too loudly and with a nervous cackle. "How you do talk."

"It's the heavenly sight of you," Joseph says, "that inspires me."

After he's gone into the house, Malinda whispers to Elizabeth, "What do you think of him?"

"Think of him?" The lye burns Elizabeth's hands. "Why should I think anything of him?"

"I only meant to find out your opinion of him."

"Are you sweet on him, Malinda?"

"I am. But don't you tell."

"No, I won't tell."

"Not even John?"

Elizabeth is scrubbing one of John's shirts on the washboard. "Would you have me keep secrets from my husband?"

"Surely there's something you've never told him."

Elizabeth scrubs the shirt more fiercely. "That's not your business."

"So there is something." Malinda cackles again and splashes soapy water from her tub onto Elizabeth's apron. "Quick, Lizzie. Tell me. What?"

"There's nothing."

"Nothing you'll tell. That's what you mean."

"Nothing," says Elizabeth. "Now leave it be."

What does Malinda know about being married? About the things husbands and wives never say to each other? She's twenty-six, but she's never made a match. Elizabeth believes it's because she's too chatty – cluck, cluck, cluck all day long like an old hen. What man could stand it, no matter how pleasing she is to look at? "Divine," Joseph said. "Blissful." Elizabeth wonders what words he has for what he saw when he spied on her and John in the woods. What if she were to tell Malinda about that – sweet Joseph hidden in the brush, watching? Would it turn her sour, or would it make him all the more exciting to her, as it has Elizabeth? He knows something about her, something meant only for her husband – the look on her face at the height of her passion – and the thought that he carries the image in his memory, revisits it at his whim, thrills her as much as it shames her. They are linked this way forever, no matter what happens from this point forward. She never meant for this to be the case, but here it is, and she doesn't know how to wash it away, or even if she cares to try.

I saw a man flirt with my mother once. I was too young to know that was what he was doing, but as I recall the incident now I can clearly see that his friendliness was not completely innocent.

We were in a Laundromat at the time, late on a Saturday evening. For a while we were the only customers – my mother and I – and then this man walked in. He was a man I didn't know, and I could tell that my mother didn't know him either. He was older than she, a big man in a tan work suit. There was a crack in the right lens of his eyeglasses. As he passed us, a soiled red bandana fell from his wooden basket. My mother picked it up. "Sir," she said in her soft voice, "you dropped this handkerchief."

"Thank you, ma'am." He took the soiled bandana from her and ducked his head as if he were embarrassed that she had been required to touch it. "You're very kind."

There are people in the world who are starved for kindness, and this man was one of them.

"You're welcome," my mother said, again in her soft voice.

She could be as timid as I, particularly in the company of strangers. I imagine that as much as she must have disliked my father's bluster, she also depended on it to make a way for her through the world. Everyone knew Roy Martin, and she was Roy Martin's wife. Without his forwardness, her voice would have been small indeed, and she would have gone unnoticed. I can imagine her shrinking like

Alice until she was so small she slipped down into the rabbit's hole.

Just recently, when I was in Lukin Township, trying to find Elizabeth Martin's grave at the Brian Cemetery, I stopped at a house to ask directions. I stood in the yard with a man I didn't know from Adam. He was drinking a bottle of beer, tending a fire that was burning in a barbecue pit. A man and woman were sitting on a deck alongside the house.

He was getting ready to grill some steaks, the first man explained.

I felt that I was intruding, that I was an outsider, suspect because of my unannounced visit and the out-of-state license plates on my car. So I said what I always did whenever I wanted to make a connection in that part of the country; I used my father's name as a password. "Do you remember Roy Martin?" I asked the man.

"Well, sure I remember Roy. He was first cousin to my dad."

"Who's your dad?"

"Raymond Inyart. I'm Bill."

I told him that I was Roy Martin's son, and he got chatty, telling me how he hunted wild turkeys on the farm where I had lived, the one that bordered his grandparents' old homeplace on the southwest corner. "Fred and Minnie's," he said. "Fred was my granddad. He was brother to your grandma, Stellie. Now let's see your mom was a . . ." He tapped the lip of the beer bottle against his teeth and tried to conjure up my mother's maiden name.

"She was a Read," I told him.

"No, she was a Knackmuhs."

I told him he was thinking of my mother's sister, Anna, who had married Richard Knackmuhs.

He looked puzzled. "I could have sworn your mom was a Knackmuhs."

I take this as a sign of the sort of impression my mother left on people who didn't know her well. *Beulah Martin? Oh yeah, she was Roy Martin's wife.* But who was she beyond that fact?

She was the woman who every morning rose at dawn to read from her Bible, to have this quiet time before my father demanded her care. She was the one who put on a baseball glove and played catch with me, even hit pop-ups and grounders so I could practice my fielding. She was the woman who baked chiffon cakes for our family get-togethers; who grew marigolds and zinnias in her flowerbeds;

who taught grade school for thirty-eight years; who worked in the laundry room at the nursing home after she retired from teaching and came home each day, the skin on her hands red and peeling; who dressed my father, bathed him, shaved him, who never uttered a single word of complaint.

On Saturday evenings she baked piecrusts for Sunday's communion service at the Church of Christ. She still had this to do that evening when we were in the Laundromat, and perhaps that's why she was in a hurry. She knew that my father, who had gone uptown to shoot the breeze with the other loafers at the pool hall, would soon return, expecting our clothes to be washed and dried and folded so we could make the ten-mile drive from town to our farm and do what had to be done before we could lie down and sleep.

"Give me a hand," my mother told me, and I helped her pull the last load of wet clothes from the washing machine and throw them into the wire cart for the trip to the row of dryers along the wall.

The dryer wouldn't work. My mother put in her dime, turned the knob, but nothing happened. "Oh, dear," she said.

The man in the work suit came over from his washing machine. "Trouble, ma'am?" he said. "A nice lady like you don't need no trouble."

My mother jiggled the dryer's knob. "It took my dime," she said, "and now it won't run. I guess I'll have to try another machine."

"Let me help you." The man moved in close to my mother and started lifting the wet clothes out of the dryer. There they were, the two of them so close their arms were touching. At one point they both reached into the tangle of wet clothes, and, when the man pulled out a wad, he also had hold of my mother's hand. "Well," he said with a grin, "stuck in my thumb and pulled out a plum." Then he gave my mother's hand a pat and let it go.

I could tell that now she was the one who was embarrassed. The wet clothes included my mother's brassieres, slips, and underpants. The man was holding these items in his hands. "These are your soft things," he said in a voice almost numb with awe. "You got to take good care of your soft lady things."

"Thank you," my mother said. "Thank you for your help."

She pushed the cart down the row of dryers to the first one, the one near the front door and the wide plate-glass window that looked out on the street. It was nearly dark, and a little rain had started to fall. I could see it in the headlights of cars as they hissed past on the wet street.

"Raining," the man said. He took a few steps in our direction. "Will you be needing a ride? I'd be glad to give you a ride."

Just then my father came through the door, and I was glad to see him. I imagine my mother must have been happy, too. "Roy," she said, and there was relief in her voice, and what I imagine now was the sound of love.

My uncle told me once that my father was my mother's only beau. I can't imagine why other men – men like the one in the Laundromat – weren't drawn toward her sweetness. Perhaps it was simply because she was so shy it was difficult for them to notice her.

I wonder whether my great-great-grandmother, Elizabeth, had a similar sweetness. Her name, if I let it, suggests as much. *Elizabeth.* The gentle glide of those four syllables.

But the opposite might have been true. She might have been harsh and resentful, bitter because John had taken her away from Kentucky, away from her mother and father. She might have longed to tell him how she dreamed of Joseph's beautiful hands, how she knew he had watched them that evening in the woods, how she was glad of it. She might have ached to say these things to John just to see how it would hurt him.

Still, perhaps Elizabeth never took any notice at all of Joseph, only knowing him as the man who would one day marry Malinda. Maybe Elizabeth was utterly devoted to John, willing to follow him wherever he might decide to take her. After all, I'm spinning their story now, inventing it as I go, and maybe I've been wrong at every turn. But how can I be wrong when really I'm the one I'm writing, the teller exposed in the telling?

Why have I chosen to create this attraction Elizabeth feels toward Joseph? Is it because I wonder in my heart of hearts whether my mother ever longed for a release from my father, whether she regretted having married him? If she ever had these feelings – any trace of them – I imagine that she pushed them down deep inside her, away from light and air, so they could never take root and grow.

I was the one who cruelly longed for another father, someone more patient, more gentle, more kind. I told my father I hated him, told him I wished I'd never been born his son, and when I said these things, I meant them, no matter how much I ached for his love.

So I'm writing an old story here, the one that began the day my father lost his hands, a story that never really ended. Despite the fact that by the time of his death we had learned to be more respectful of each other, there remains to this day the hurtful memory of how we cheapened love with our rage. All along our bond was meant to be sacred, but we were too selfish, too angry, too weak. And what's left to me, the only one still alive, is a bottomless desire to go back, to make amends, to rescue us from anger.

So I imagine Elizabeth threatened by this desire she has for a man so unlike her husband – no more than a boy, really, this Joseph. She thinks she could lose herself at any moment, lose the life she's imagined is hers. There's William and Sarah, playing with cornhusk dolls one evening by the fire, and Joseph turns another page of his book, and Elizabeth thinks, *Oh, my.* She feels herself slipping away from her children and from John, who's out in the yard sharpening an ax blade at the grindstone.

What is it that makes us long for other worlds? What hunger? Is it our common flaw to always believe we could have other lives, better lives? Is it this – this greed that keeps us hurtling toward one another and away?

Each night my mother knelt to say her prayers. I came upon her once when I was grown, on an evening when I had spoken sharp words to her. She was seventy-five and had started to have the small strokes that slowly over the next three years would rob her of memory and reasoning and, finally, language. I had become annoyed with her on this evening because I had discovered that the neighborhood children, whom she had allowed in her house, had stolen money from her, had even stolen blank checks and forged her signature. I had yet to acknowledge the fact that my mother, because of the strokes, because of her natural trust and timidity, was blameless, not to be held to account. "How could you let this happen?" I had snapped at her, and then, before going to bed, I had come out to apologize.

She was kneeling by the sofa in the living room, her hands folded and her head bowed. Her hair was hanging in a braid down her back. Her bare heels, the soles of her feet, stuck out from beneath the hem of her white gown. She wasn't saying anything, but her eyes were closed, and I knew that she was speaking from her heart to the God she had always believed would care for her.

For what did she give thanks? The breath she drew? The house that sheltered her? The food she ate? Did she give thanks for me, who had spoken sharply to her? For the years she had spent with my father, even though he had been a man of temper, despite the fact that he had demanded so much from her? I understood, as I watched her humble and silent prayer, that she had always been willing to sacrifice the self in order to make room for others, to celebrate their brilliant lights or to brighten the days of those who suffered torments they couldn't manage to escape. If there was any plan to the universe at all, I decided, it surely had been God's intent that my mother marry my father, that she be there with him after he lost his hands, to help him through his years of rage. I doubted that she had ever considered him a burden. I imagined that she would forgive my sharp words, had already forgiven them, no doubt. She had told me for as long as I could remember that time was all it took to heal a hurt, that everything, no matter how grim, always looked better come tomorrow. "Count your blessings," she always said. She told me this again and again during my troubled teen years, when I was full of the rage that I had learned from my father. There were nights when I was so tormented I had trouble sleeping. "Count your blessings," she told me then. Sometimes she sat on the edge of my bed, watching over me, soothing me with her presence.

"Don't think bad thoughts," she said. "Think of all the good things in your life."

She didn't deserve the end that she came to – aphasic in a nursing home, tied to her chair to keep her from roaming away as she was apt to do. I used to loosen her restraints and sit beside her and hold her hand. My cousin tells me that when she and her parents, my mother's sister, Anna, and her husband, Richard, came to the nursing home to visit my mother, they all stood in a circle, hands linked, and recited the Lord's Prayer. My mother, who had lost the ability to make sentences, who could only mumble sounds and grunts, was able to say the words – "Our father, who art in Heaven" – all the way to the prayer's end. So deep, so lasting, was her faith that even the brain's breakdown could never take it away from her.

So ultimately it's faith I long for, faith I want to give Elizabeth, faith that we can stand on level ground and hunger no more.

Perhaps she says to Joseph, "I know it was you. Watching. That evening in the woods."

Joseph lowers his book, lets it lie open on his lap. "Watching," he says.

"Yes," says Elizabeth. "Me and John. You picked the leaves from me, and I smelled the woods on you. That's how I knew."

"You and John picked blackberries."

"Yes."

"And you had leaves in your hair, twigs stuck to your dress."

"Yes," she says, enchanted with the way their voices have hushed until their words are the slightest puffs of air. She knows that he's admitting it to her, his presence that day in the woods, and she believes that everything depends on what she decides to do next – every bit of her future. She doesn't know how far she'll travel. She doesn't know about Illinois or the child, Nancy, growing now in her womb, the child who will one day rest beside her in the Brian Cemetery, atop the hill in Lukin Township in the shade of the hickory trees. She doesn't know anything about the generations to whom she's giving birth, or how I'll find her one day, touch her fallen grave marker, run my fingers over the etched grooves that used to say her name. All she knows is the ache in her heart. "Go outside," she says to William and Sarah. "Run out and show your dolls to your father."

When they're gone, she thinks, she'll go to Joseph, and she'll take his hands, and she'll hold them to her face and let herself go from this world, let her secret desires come winging from her body like quail lifting up from cover, rising in flight.

But when she finally moves to him, when he lifts his face to look at her, she's overwhelmed with how young he is, how the tremor in his lips, the blinking of his eyes, remind her of John the morning he woke from the cholera, come back from the dead, alive to birdsong. She watched him sip water, leaning toward him, lips parted, as if she, too, were parched and thirsting for drink.

She starts to cry. She moves her hand toward Joseph. Then she stops and listens to John's voice rising outside, making a show over William and Sarah's dolls. "My goodness, gracious sakes alive," he says over the singing of the ax blade on the grindstone. "Would you look at them pretties? What's their names?"

"Mama," says Sarah.

"And Daddy," says William.

Later, when Elizabeth puts the children to bed, she'll take the dolls from them, hold them side by side and feel the dry cornhusks with her hands.

But now she's holding her hand between her and Joseph. He won't look at her. His voice is so hushed she can barely hear it.

"It wasn't me," he says. Already she feels the next step she'll take, toward the door, toward the light outside, toward her husband and children, toward the earth turning over beneath her feet. "I swear, Elizabeth. It was never me."

4
One I Love, Two I Love

The facts are these:

On February 28, 1848, in Lukin Township, Clarissa Ridgley married Jonathan Inyart. Eleven months later, on January 13, 1849, she gave birth to their only child, Mary Ann. Jonathan died soon after from summer complaint, a common and dangerous digestive illness of the time that usually struck children. Clarissa and Mary Ann went to live with Clarissa's parents until August 1, 1856, when she married William Bell. Mr. Bell, a widower, had a child of his own, a daughter, as fortune would have it, named Mary Ann. Clarissa left her own Mary Ann to stay with her grandparents and moved a few miles east to Mr. Bell's farm. Never again did she live under the same roof as her daughter.

Because my mother and father were older, I often imagined that they weren't my real parents, that someone had abandoned me, like Moses left in the bulrushes, and this aging couple had found me and taken me in. For that reason alone, the story of Mary Ann Inyart compels me. I keep imagining that she must have felt betrayed, deserted, rejected for another little girl who shared her name.

Deb tells me that I should be careful not to assume too much. "Maybe Mary Ann was happy to stay with her grandparents," she argues. "Or maybe Clarissa didn't take her because she and Mr. Bell couldn't support her. Maybe it was just a matter of economics. Maybe Clarissa went to visit Mary Ann all the time, and everyone was happy."

These are all, of course, plausible scenarios. Last night, on a news program, I saw the story of a couple who had seventeen children. When the city condemned their house, the parents, unable to afford other housing, divided the children among various family members. Economic necessity sometimes forces families apart; this was particularly true at the time of Clarissa Ridgley, when parents often sent their children off to work as farm hands or housemaids.

So Deb is right; maybe Clarissa made the decision that she did and everyone was happy with it. Deb was an only child for ten years, but her parents were very young, having had her when they were both in their early twenties. She never grew up, as I did, with the haunting dread that her parents would die and leave her an orphan. When she considers Clarissa's story, she thinks first of this young widow, forced now by her husband's death to live again in her mother's house, to give up whatever independence her marriage had brought her. Deb and I married when she was seventeen, and she'll be the first to admit that, when she met me, she saw a chance to get away from home, where she felt imprisoned by her mother's nagging and her forbidding manner. She brings her dread of entrapment to bear on Clarissa's story, just as I bring my own fear of abandonment.

"And Clarissa must have been lonely," she says. "Six years without a husband."

Deb admits that she sometimes has dreams that I've died and left her alone for the rest of her life. She sees her widowed mother and how bleak her life is. She doesn't want to think of Clarissa in a similar situation, so she imagines that she found happiness with William Bell. I hope that's the case, too, but still I can't stop thinking about Mary Ann and how she must have felt in her heart of hearts to live apart from her mother.

When I imagine her now, it's a summer day in 1862, and she's just come out of the woods with her aunt Sally, whose given name is Sarah, their pails full of blackberries. The men are working hay in the meadow behind the house. The sun is high, and it glints off the tines of the pitchforks as the men toss the cut timothy grass into stacks. The forks whisk through the timothy, making a noise that reminds Mary Ann of the whispers she heard from her bed the night her mother announced that she was going to marry William Bell. "I've been a widow nearly six years," she said. "It's lonely without a husband. I can tell you that."

Mary Ann and Sally are some one hundred yards away from the men, half-hidden behind the honeysuckle that grows along the tree line. "Crouch down." Mary Ann grabs Sally by the sleeve of her shirtwaist and pulls her to her knees. "They don't even know we're here. We're like spies."

"They're just bringing in the hay." Sally's bucket has tipped over, and she's trying to gather the berries that have spilled. Her fingers are stained purple from the juice. "What's so interesting about that?"

Mary Ann loves everything about men. She loves the way her uncle Benton keeps his wide-brimmed hat straight on his head even as he pitches the hay, and the way her uncle Alfred, Sally's husband, wipes his face on his shirt sleeve. And she feels herself go woozy – that's the way she imagines her mother saying it, *woozy* – when she sees Henry Martin, Sally's brother. He's stripped himself to the waist, and Mary Ann can't stop looking at his bare chest, his arms corded with muscle.

"There's Henry." She whispers this to Sally. "Look at him. Oh, would you just look? He makes me woozy."

"Mary Ann, you're a scandal," says Sally.

"Tell me all about how it happens." The sun is shining on Henry's broad chest. "You know, between women and men."

"I'll tell you no such thing. You're not but thirteen."

"Thirteen's a woman. Some girls have got babies by then."

"Well, you don't need to be thinking of following suit."

"Mama said it was lonely without a man. She waited six years after Papa died. 'Six lonely years.'" Mary Ann puts the back of her hand to her forehead and tosses her head back the way she imagines her mother did the night she said she would marry William Bell. "'Would you have me suffer an eternity?'"

"Don't make fun of your mother."

"She never loved me," Mary Ann says. Then she comes out from behind the honeysuckle and goes running through the cut hay.

Maybe Deb is imagining the moment when William Bell first hints to Clarissa that they might make a pair. Maybe it happens at the Ridgley farm, where he's come to help with the threshing. At noon the men wash the wheat chaff from their hands and arms. Some of them douse their heads in the horse tank and come to the table, their hair slicked back as sleek as seals. Clarissa thinks of babies – their bright eyes, the way their skin pinkens when it's washed, its sweet smell. She's only had a chance to be a mother once. Jonathan died, and here she is nearly thirty, feeling that her best years are slipping by her. In a wink she'll be as old as her mother, Mary. She'll be an old widow woman, wizened and humpbacked, relying on the kindness of her neighbors.

She likes the way the men become polite and soft-spoken in the company of women. They say, "Please, Miss," when she asks them whether they'd like a powder biscuit, and "Thank you, Miss," when she pours them another glass of tea.

After they've eaten, William lingers outside while the other men go back to the field. He's there in the yard when Clarissa comes out to throw the table scraps to the hogs.

"It was all fine eats," he says. "Did you make them biscuits?"

"No," Clarissa says. "Mother did."

"I bet you make some fine biscuits yourself."

"I learned how," she says, "back when I set up house. Now Mother won't hardly let me touch a rolling pin."

"I'd let you make biscuits for me, Clarissa."

William is looking down at his feet. Clarissa can see his pink scalp where the hair is thinning. She knows he's trying to play the spark with her, and he's so shy about it she finds his clumsy attempt endearing. His wife has only been gone a year – cholera – and this must feel so odd to him.

Clarissa thinks of Jonathan lying those three months in his bed, death coming to him, and she wishes for the umpteenth time that she could have done something to save him. She made poultices from tansy leaves, steeped bloodroot in milk, made syrup from rhubarb, but nothing worked. He went away from her, and now here she is looking into William's eyes. He seems so afraid, she imagines that if she said, "Boo," he'd crumple to the ground. How helpless a man is, she thinks, how sweet, when he's trying to tell a woman that he needs her.

"How do you like your biscuits?" she asks him. "With melted butter? Honey?"

"Oh, I like my biscuits just about any way."

"I can make them that way." She takes a step toward him. "Believe me, I can. If I ever get the chance."

"I'd like to give you that chance," he says, and she knows that, in their awkward way, they've just agreed to marry.

My own proposal to Deb was nearly as haphazard. We had been

dating barely a month, a courtship that started in the spring of 1975 when I was finishing my sophomore year at the community college in Olney. Deb was about to graduate from high school, and I suppose we were both at pivotal moments, when we would take a step this way or that and everything would change for us. I was making plans to attend Eastern Illinois University in Charleston; Deb was imagining that she would keep working at Burger Chef until she could get a job at the shoe factory or the garment factory and make enough money to finally move out of her parents' house.

And then one Saturday night I walked into Burger Chef. It was late, and the restaurant was nearly empty, just a few people like me and my friends, hanging out because there was nothing better to do. I remember so well the feeling I had in those days – a nervous energy, a restless expectation. My friends and I would cruise Main Street, making the turnaround at the east end in the Kentucky Fried Chicken parking lot, and then head back west to the bowling alley or the skating rink, anxious for something to happen. And, of course, what we hoped for most of all was that some girls somewhere would fall for us. It was spring, the air finally warm after winter's long freeze, the scent of the thawing earth all around us, the sweet perfume of lilac. We drove down Main Street with the car windows down, the tape deck playing something throbbing – Deep Purple, Alice Cooper – or something sweet with yearning – the *American Graffiti* soundtrack, which had started the fifties revival – or something even more sentimental – Bread or Jim Croce. By evening's end our bravado would be gone, and we would make the quiet drive home.

I had been in the Burger Chef before when Deb was working, and I had noted her bright smile and the friendly way she had with the customers. Her face was alive – that smile, those green eyes, a laugh that charmed me, not to mention the smoothest skin I had ever seen and a blond ponytail that bounced against her back as she moved about behind the counter. Her vitality won me.

One day, when it came time to pay my bill, I was a penny short. "I'm sorry," I said, embarrassed.

"Don't worry," she told me. "I'll pay it." And she took a penny from her apron pocket and dropped it into the till.

That Saturday night I finally worked up the nerve to talk to her. I

leaned on the counter and tried to think of something flirtatious
to say, something to let her know I was interested but nothing that
would make her think I was one of those dangerous guys her parents
had surely cautioned her to avoid. Earlier in the evening I had heard
some people at the bowling alley talking about a late-night party out
in the country by Noble – one of those beer blasts in a field – and
though I had no desire to go there, now it was the only ammunition
I could muster. "I hear there's a big party tonight," I said, trying not
to seem lecherous. "Maybe we could go."

"We don't even know each other." Deb was sweet but timid. Later
she admitted that she didn't want me to think that she was, in her
words, "an easy-sleazy." "I can't go to a party with you."

"We could get to know each other," I said. Where was the generous
girl who had been so quick with the penny? Couldn't she see I was
harmless?

"I don't know," she said, and then her attention was diverted to
something in the parking lot. "Hey, someone's taking my car."

It turned out to be her father, driving the car to the filling station
next door and then bringing it back. When he came into the Burger
Chef to tell Deb what he had done, I went to the booth where my
friends were sitting, thinking that I had lost my chance.

Our lives can turn on the smallest of things. In my case it was a
piece of ice as big around as the end of my little finger. If Deb hadn't
thrown it at me after her father left, I may have never spoken to her
again. But because she did – "I had to do something," she told me
later. "I couldn't stand to think that you might walk out of there" – I
went back to the counter and said, "We could go out next weekend,
maybe out to Art's Truck Stop. I like to get coffee there. Maybe we
could just sit around and talk."

And she said that would be fine with her.

The night of our date, we did what I had promised; we drove out
to Art's Truck Stop, and over coffee we talked. Our conversation, if
anyone had preserved it on tape, would probably embarrass me now.
In those days I could be earnest and impassioned. I could rail against
the capitalists, denounce the conservatives, quote Whitman and
Thoreau. At the drop of a hat, I could turn sentimental. I could recite
passages from Kahlil Gibran's *The Prophet*, Rod McKuen poems,
pop-song lyrics. I thought such sources scripture when it came to

love. I could even quote from the Bible. "There is no fear in love," I easily might have said, "but perfect love casteth out fear."

Part of me wants to be ashamed of such blathering now, but another part – the one that remembers what it was to be young – feels sweetly seduced. How passionate we were then – how unaware that generations and generations before us had been passionate, too.

I told Deb that I was an only child, that my father had lost his hands in a farming accident when I was barely a year old. I told her he wore hooks now, that he and my mother were in their sixties, that my biggest fear, when I was growing up, was that they would die and leave me an orphan. I said I believed in living a spiritual life, in being kind and good. I said, "It's the first thing I noticed about you. The way you treat people."

She told me that when she was young, her mother had refused to let her grow her hair long. "I always had to have a pixie cut," she said, "because it was easier to take care of. Straight hair, round face: it wasn't a pretty sight." Her mother, a child during the Depression, valued practicality over fashion. She bought sturdy oxford shoes for Deb instead of penny loafers and patent-leather Mary Janes. She sewed together polyester slacks that would last instead of buying Deb Levi jeans that would eventually fade and wear thin. "Now I've got my own job," Deb told me, "and I can buy whatever I want."

Her problems with her mother ran much deeper than arguments over clothes. In her mother's house she felt imprisoned, never allowed to be herself. She couldn't even have privacy. Her mother refused to let her have a lock on her bedroom door, insisted that it stay open. The only place in the house where Deb could be alone was the bathroom, which did have a lock, but even then her mother would bang on the door and shout, "What are you doing in there?" She was a woman driven by fear and paranoia and a powerful desire to control her surroundings. And Deb's father was reluctant to involve himself with his family. He was willing to spend his time puttering around in the garage, sacrificing the house and what went on there to Deb's mother.

These were the sorts of things we told each other that night at the truck stop, and when I think of these two people now, the people we once were, I feel a great tenderness toward them. There they sit at a Formica-covered table in the corner of a truck stop out on Highway

50, miles from town, far away from the houses to which they'll soon return and the people there – their parents – who have no idea that their very presence has started to determine what will happen next, who do not know that their children lie awake in the dark, dreaming about leaving them.

"The times are always so beautiful when we are together," Deb said to me in a letter that I've saved from those days. "One day has gone by and I feel as though it has been weeks since I've seen you."

"When did you know I was the one?" I ask her now from time to time.

"I knew it then," she says. "That night."

I knew it, too. I knew that we were connected in a profound way that was, perhaps, beyond words or understanding. Or maybe we were just so restless, so fearful, so anxious, that we clung to each other, barely able to believe our luck.

One night, as we sat on a blanket at the farm my father still owned though we had moved into town – a farm first owned by Henry Martin – I said, "What would you say if I asked you to marry me?"

Deb didn't hesitate. "I'd say yes," she told me, and I knew my life had changed forever.

So when I think now of Mary Ann running through the hayfield toward Henry on that day in 1862, I already know what they don't; they're in the middle of a love story. I wonder whether Henry has even paid her any mind, only to know her as his sister's niece. After all, he's nineteen, and his head is full these days with the talk of war.

He knows a boy from Wabash County who mustered in the summer before, when he was seventeen. He marched with Grant into Kentucky and took Fort Henry and Fort Donelson and then moved on to Shiloh in Tennessee and took it, too. Henry has listened to the Ridgleys as they've read aloud the newspaper accounts of the battles, and he's dreamed himself in those places amidst the cannon fire and the drums and the pounding of horses' hooves. He's seen boys there in Lukin on their way to Sumner or Lancaster to join up, and he's been ashamed for them to see him, still hoeing corn and pitching hay when there's a war to be fought, gray-coats to be killed. Here he is now, working with the old man, Alfred – only thirty-three, he seems ancient to Henry, who notes his slumped shoulders and the gray already starting to speckle his beard – and the objector, Benton, twenty-one, who leads singing at the Gilead Methodist Church and believes killing to be wrong, no matter the circumstances. "What about if those rebs came up here and killed your ma?" Henry said to Benton just that morning in the hayfield, and Benton quoted scripture back at him: "Vengeance is mine; thus sayeth the Lord."

Henry wants to go to war, but his father, John, has forbidden it. "I lost one child," he's told Henry. "I'll not be losing another."

It's been less than eight months since Henry's sister Nancy died. She was only twenty-one, and the typhoid took her. Out of John and Elizabeth Martin's eight children, she's the only one they've lost, a blessing that astounds them, given the fact that so many of their neighbors have put young'uns in the ground. Just look at the Ridgleys, six lost and Alfred's wife to boot. They've buried them all atop the hill on the east edge of their farm, a spot they've cleared of timber and seeded with bluegrass. Often Henry, because the Martins hire themselves out to the Ridgleys from time to time, mows the grass at the cemetery. He swings his scythe from side to side, uses his hand sickle around the ornate gravestones: the ones topped with cornices, the ones that have angels etched on them or hands with fingers pointing up to Heaven. He knows the names by heart: Charles, Sarah Ann, Eliza, Richard, Mary Jane, Sintha, Elizabeth. His sister Sally has married into this family, but he wonders whether Alfred really loves her or whether he simply needs a woman to look after his children. It's the Ridgleys' way to get whatever they want: wives, land, fancy tombstones, another family even, if Clarissa's any gauge. She traded in her daughter for another one of the same name, and now here she comes – the brat, Mary Ann – tromping through the hay, not caring a whit that she's scattering blackberries from her pail.

"Aw, look at you," Henry says. "Throwing good berries to the birds."

Mary Ann reaches into her pail and chants as she drops berries to the ground. "One I love, two I love, three I love, I say." She holds a berry up to Henry's lips. "Four I love with all my heart." He keeps his mouth closed. "Four I love with all my heart," she says again, this time with more force, and he opens his mouth and lets her lay the berry on his tongue. "Is it sweet?" she says to him.

"It's sweet," he says.

"That's because I picked it." She smiles at him, and he notices for the first time that she's growing up, that she'll be a pretty woman like her mother, that she'll know exactly what to do to snag a man.

That evening Clarissa and William come for supper. They have the children with them: Mary Ann, whom they've started calling Annie; William Jr.; and the three Clarissa has brought into the world – Marion and Amy and John. The women dish up the food and set it on the table while the children play bullpen in the yard and the men talk horses out at the stable. Soon someone will call them in to eat.

Annie is fifteen. She's wearing a tight-waisted dress that shows off the curve of her hips, her full breasts. Clarissa has helped her curl the ends of her hair, and Mary Ann, though she would never admit it, adores the honeyed spirals bouncing along Annie's slender neck. She flits about the kitchen, chattering on and on about the box supper at the Gilead Church that coming Sunday.

"I'm making a chiffon cake," she says. "Mama's helping me."

Mary Ann takes a dish of boiled cabbage from her and wrinkles her nose at the smell.

"Is there some special beau you're hoping buys it?" Grandma Ridgley asks.

"Might be," Annie says. "I'm not saying."

"Chiffon." Her grandma shakes her head. "I swan. That's fancy."

Grandma Ridgley has told Mary Ann that she'll teach her how to bake a pound cake. How boring, Mary Ann thinks: sugar and flour and water and shortening. She imagines the chiffon cakes she saw her mother make before she married Mr. Bell: the satiny smooth batter, how she folded the egg whites into it, how light and sweet.

"It's not that hard," Mary Ann says.

Annie puts her hands on her hips. "I suppose you could make one."

"No, I couldn't make one." Mary Ann knows she's trying to force her mother to feel sorry for her. "Not unless Mama helped me."

"Why, Mary Ann," Clarissa says. "I never knew you to take an interest in such things."

Mary Ann wants to tell her that she's becoming a young lady, that she has interest in all sorts of things. She wants to tell her how the sight of Henry Martin can make her woozy. But she can't without validating the very thing that took her mother away from her – the desire for a man. She can't let her mother know that she's exactly like her.

A few years ago Deb's mom started giving her keepsakes: letters she and her husband, Loren, had written each other before they were married; a wooden plate someone had made for their wedding, *Wilma and Loren* hand-painted above a dove and a sprig of daisies, the date, *April 30, 1955*, inscribed below; a silver platter from their twenty-fifth anniversary.

Deb was embarrassed to accept such items. "Oh, don't you want to keep them?" she finally said to her mother.

"No, go ahead," Wilma told her. "You'll end up with them anyway."

Loren had been gone two years. Early one morning in 1993, he had stepped from his bedroom into the hallway and fallen to the floor, dead from a heart attack. Wilma had been sleeping on the couch in the living room, as was her habit those days since Loren, afflicted with sleep apnea, was often a difficult bed companion. I imagine her waking to the sound of his falling and finding him collapsed there in the hallway. Her house must have seemed like a strange place to her then and for the two years she remained there before moving into town. Though the Regulator clock still ticked along in the bedroom, and the sunlight came through the living room's picture window each afternoon, it must have felt so odd to be alone there, without the man she had loved nearly forty years.

Perhaps she thinks back now to the summer of 1975, when Deb and I married without her blessing, and she understands exactly why we did it. I like to believe that in her widowhood she recalls the power of love and how once we fall under its spell all we can do is follow it to its end, no matter the voices telling us to have more sense.

"How will you live?" Wilma said when Deb told her we were going to marry and then move to Charleston so I could finish college.

"I'll work," Deb told her, "and so will Lee."

My parents had already agreed to go ahead and pay my tuition.

"Work at what?" Wilma was wiping off the kitchen table, around which Deb and I sat. Loren was in the living room reading the newspaper.

"Something will come along," Deb said.

Wilma scrubbed furiously at a stubborn spot on the table. Suddenly she placed her hands flat on the table and leaned toward us. "Well, I won't sign for you. I'll tell you that."

The wedding date we had chosen, August 10, was a week before Deb's eighteenth birthday. "I'll get Daddy to do it," she said.

"Did you hear that, Loren?" Wilma shouted into the living room, where Loren was hidden behind the newspaper he had spread in front of his face. "Are you going to sign for her?"

His voice, when he answered, was quiet but sure. "I guess I will," he said. And that was that.

Perhaps he remembered, better than Wilma, their own anguished yearnings when they weren't much older than Deb and I were then and everyone was telling them not to do anything foolish.

Loren was a private in the army, stationed first at Fort Leonard Wood in Missouri and then later at Fort Sam Houston in San Antonio. He enlisted in 1954, when he was twenty and Wilma was nineteen. Their letters to each other, from his time in the army, are filled with talk of marriage. In one Wilma reports how her sister warned her not to marry him when he was home on leave: "Now don't get married when he's home," her sister said. "You better wait until he's out, and then both of you will be happier."

Wilma writes to Loren: "Darling, of course I doubt if my folks and your folks wants us to, but I know what our mothers said on the Monday we was up there. My mother and your mother both said we can only tell them and the rest is up to them."

In a letter from Fort Sam Houston postmarked August 10, exactly twenty years before Deb and I would marry, Loren writes to Wilma about the length of his time there: fourteen weeks. "After I find more about it," he says, "I will tell you just how long it will be before we can get married. It will be as soon as possible, and I think you know I mean it. I will get an emergency leave and come home and get you and bring you back with me."

A few months later, in December, he writes about his parents' objections to his plans to marry Wilma, objections he quickly overcomes with his fervent desires:

Honey, I called home tonight and talked to mother, and she asked if we was planning on getting married when I come home for Christmas, and

I told her that we had no plans, then she said she would rather for us not to. Honey, every one says that we should wait, and we both know it would be better if we did, but I don't know if we can wait, I don't think we can. I love and want you with all my heart. Sweetheart, I wish that we could be married right now, but we are going to wait at least one more week and a half. I love you sweetheart, and I don't care who knows it. I long for you every night darling, I won't be happy until you are in my arms again.

He didn't marry Wilma that Christmas, waiting a few months more. He married her in April and promptly got his orders for Frankfurt, Germany, where he spent the rest of his enlistment working as a technician in a dental clinic. Wilma kept living with her parents in Illinois, a married woman now, but with no man to show for it.

After Jonathan died, Clarissa did the only thing she could; she came home to her mother and father. She brought her baby, Mary Ann, and right away it felt as if she were handing the child over to them. How they doted on their little Mary. And Clarissa, sinking into the blackness of her grief, was glad not to have to worry about caring for the baby. Six years went by, and as Mary Ann grew older, she came to look more and more like Jonathan – the same slender nose, the curl in her dark hair, the heavy-lidded eyes that always made her look sleepy, and oh so beautiful, and oh so full of mystery. She resembled Jonathan so much it was sometimes painful for Clarissa to look at her.

"You're a little Indian girl," Grandpa Ridgley often told her. "We stole you away from the Shawnees."

What foolishness. But what else was there to say, since at first no one wanted to tell Mary Ann about her father and how he had died? "I'm an Indian," she often told people, and they agreed that she was a wild one all right, a real hellion, so different from Clarissa, who spent her days shuffling about the house, hardly making a sound. She sewed, washed clothes, made lye soap, did whatever chore her mother gave her, glad at first to have someone tell her how to get through the days. "Yes, ma'am," she said to her mother as if she were once again a girl.

When all the work was done, she sometimes sat in her room and idly plucked the strings on the fiddle that Jonathan used to play. She pulled her rocking chair close to the window and held the fiddle on her lap. The rosewood body gleamed in the sunlight. She watched Mary Ann scampering about in the farmyard – trying to ride baby pigs, to catch guineas – and Clarissa was surprised to suddenly find herself crying. She cried because the black-haired girl, laughing and squealing, seemed so strange to her. And she cried because she knew how difficult it would be to ever feel such joy herself as long as she lived in her parents' house, where it was so painfully clear that she was a widow.

So when William Bell finally gets around to officially proposing – "Tying the knot good and proper," he says – she doesn't hesitate. She can already imagine the changes she'll make at his house – the new curtains she'll sew, the hollyhocks she'll plant by the door, the quilt she'll make to cover them in their bed. She dreams of the new clothes she'll sew for the boy and girl, William Jr. and Mary Ann. She imagines waking them each morning and helping them dress, brushing Mary Ann's hair. If she marries William, she can see herself stepping back into the life that she and Jonathan would have had if he hadn't died.

"I've been so lonely," she tells her mother. "I'm not sure I even knew it until that day William was here to help with the threshing."

"What about Mary Ann?" her mother says. "*Your* Mary Ann."

"She's happy here," Clarissa says, and she knows she won't even ask Mary Ann whether she wants to go with her. She can't afford to, because if the answer is yes, Clarissa will never be able to escape Jonathan's death. Mary Ann – *her* Mary Ann – will always remind her of the way her life stopped those six years. And how will she be able to lie down with another man if Mary Ann, who looks so much like Jonathan, moves through the same house? "Happy," Clarissa says again, trying to convince herself it's true.

And maybe it is. Maybe Mary Ann, for a while, thinks nothing at all of the fact that her mother no longer lives with her. There's her uncle Benton, who lets her sit on his lap by the fire in the evening while he reads his Bible. The Bible has a drawing in it of Mary anointing the feet of Christ. She kneels on a rug, her fingers dipping into a clay bowl, Christ's naked foot resting on her thigh. Her long hair trails down her arms, falls over her bosom. "That's your name," Benton says, and he points to the word *Mary.*

Mary Ann likes the way she feels when Benton smiles at her – protected, safe, warm there by the fire. Later, her uncle Alfred tucks her into bed. He lets her open his watch, teaches her to tell the time. He keeps the watch in the pocket of his vest at the end of a gold chain. Mary Ann dreams of all things golden as she falls asleep: the watch chain, the wheat ripening in the fields, the honeycomb her grandfather finds sometimes in the high hollow of a tree.

"Sweet dreams," her uncle tells her, and she falls asleep to the gentle drone of voices, her grandparents and her uncles speaking softly because their darling Mary Ann – their little princess – has gone to bed.

Her favorite story is the one of the sleeping beauty who pricked her finger on a spindle and slept for a hundred years until a prince kissed her and she awoke. At first Mary Ann imagines that her father will come back, that one day she'll wake and find him sitting on her bed. She imagines him playing the fiddle, the one her mother used to let her pluck. Then, as she grows older, her father, whom she has only imagined, having no image of him, only the gleaming rosewood of the fiddle, the horsehair string of the bow, recedes. She's thirteen, and her father is gone, and her mother, and she dreams of boys – boys like Henry Martin, who she hopes will buy her cake, even if it is a wretched pound cake, at the Gilead box social come Sunday.

Deb and I married on a Sunday afternoon. I went to church with my parents that morning and came home with them and sat at their table as I had for nearly twenty years. It seems such a short time, now that I've lived twenty-six years beyond it, now that I've spent a longer time on my own than I did under my parents' care.

My mother was sixty-five that day in 1975; my father was sixty-two. They had fallen in love twenty-four years earlier. My mother was an old-maid schoolteacher, living at home with her parents; my father was a bachelor farmer, caring for his aged mother. How happy I am that they found each other. I can't bear the thought that they might have lived out their lives never having shared a passage through the years. That passage was pocked with pitfalls, but my parents' years together contained much joy as well. When I think of them now, I remember them as partners – helpmeets, in the language of Genesis.

I think of them most poignantly in spring, when Deb and I plant our vegetable garden, set out begonias and coleus and daisies, watch our rosebushes burst into flower. Evenings, as my parents often did, we work in our garden, tend our flower beds. We check on the bud swell of our red oak, note the peonies growing up from their winter's sleep, the blackberry canes green with new growth. What I feel is what my parents must have felt with each turn of the season – thankful to walk the earth with each other, their union easing them through the unforgiving march of time.

When I think of my parents, I think of swans, who mate for life, each partner devoted to the other. I think of my mother and father working side by side all those years, tending gardens, farming their eighty acres, synchronizing their rhythms with those of the planet. I think of them each time I watch rosebuds open, tomatoes bloom, blackberries set fruit – all things moving according to the seasons. I watch the slender branches of our red-tipped photinias sway in the wind. Each branch moves of its own accord, but because the photinias are so thick, so lush, what I see is a wave, an undulation, a singular swell and ebb that repeats itself.

That Sunday in 1975 my parents were nearing the end of their time together. They had only seven years left to them. Deb and I were at our beginning, and now I can admit what we didn't know then: we were just kids; we had no idea what it meant to be married, to be like the swans, like my mother and father, devoted for a lifetime. We didn't know, and still don't, the length of our journey and all it will ask of us. When I think back to the people we were that day – young and naive – I feel a tender pity. There's so much we don't know. But mostly I feel love – love for the fact that we've found each other, love for all our hope and courage and foolishness.

In our wedding photo, the one the newspaper will print, we're standing outside the church in front of a bed of cleyera and spruce and sumac. I'm wearing a cream-colored suit that my father gave me the money to buy, a red rose pinned to my lapel. Deb has on a dress that her mother sewed from polyester crepe, white with an empire waist and double-layered sleeves. Deb's hand rests in the crook of my elbow. One moment more, while the photographer holds us still. Then we'll move. We'll step from the frame and into the years. Deb has a 1975 penny in her shoe, a penny her father gave her for luck.

The afternoon of the Gilead box social is glorious. And why shouldn't it be? Mary Ann thinks, in love suddenly with the way the sunlight splinters through the treetops in the grove beside the church. The men have laid planks across barrels, and the women have covered them with oilcloths. The boxes are there among them, Annie's chiffon cake and Mary Ann's pound cake. The women have carried in food as well: smoked ham, dried pumpkin, cornbread, apple butter, watermelon and tomatoes from their gardens. After everyone has eaten, the bidding on the boxes will begin. Then the couples, the young boys and girls, will sit together and enjoy the cakes and pies.

Annie's box is tied shut with a bright pink ribbon that Mary Ann imagines her mother bought from a pack peddler. No one's supposed to know which box is whose except the preacher, who will run the bidding, but Annie has made a point of showing hers to Mary Ann, fussing over the pink ribbon, and to Henry, who is standing now with Benton and Alfred over by the horses, talking, no doubt, about the war. What else do they pay any mind to these days, even here on Sunday when everything is so lovely – the sunlight and the boxes so prettily made up with ribbons and lace. Even the horses' soft nickering fills Mary Ann with joy. Across the road a field of timothy grass, still uncut, stirs in the breeze. She remembers how only a few days before she ran through the cut hay to Henry. She recalls how she put the blackberry in his mouth, touched his lips, his tongue. She wants to go to him now and do the same thing, wants to stop him from talking about rifles and cannons and bayonets, wants to take his hand, hold it in hers until he's calm, until what he feels coming from the heat of her skin is stronger than anything he can imagine about the war.

But just then her mother takes her by both hands and dances her around in a circle while the other women, startled, watch their happy jig. "Oh, Mary Ann," Clarissa says. "Isn't it the most wonderful day?"

Clarissa has done her hair in soft, loopy curls, so different from the other women – from Sally and Grandma Ridgley and Henry's mother, Elizabeth, all of whom have their hair parted down the middle and pinned up in knots at the napes of their necks. Mary Ann loves the way her mother's curls bounce as she dances. "It is," she says. "Oh, Mother. It really is."

Then they stop, and they squeeze each other's hands, and something about that moment – perhaps it's the fact that they realize that they've just made a sight of themselves, two little fools bursting into dance, or perhaps it's nothing they can identify at all – makes them see, without having to admit it, how very much alike they are.

"You're hoping Henry buys your cake, aren't you?" Clarissa leans forward until her forehead touches Mary Ann's. Mary Ann nods, pleased to bask in her mother's warmth, to feel a curl brush ever so lightly against her face. "Have you told him which one it is?" Clarissa says.

"No," says Mary Ann. "Annie told him about hers."

"Annie's older." They're talking in whispers now, telling secrets. "She's brazen. Tell me which box is yours."

"It's the one with the dried asters on it."

"From Grandma's garden," Clarissa says. "All right. You leave everything to me."

Mary Ann must be happy to let her mother think that, when it comes to boys, she's shy. She doesn't dare tell her about the day in the hayfield when she put the blackberry into Henry's mouth. But she's frightened, too. What if Henry doesn't bid on her box? What if he chooses Annie's instead? Oh, she knows there might be other boys. There might be years and years of boys. It isn't even about that, and she may or may not understand this. Perhaps she only feels it – this thin shiver somewhere in her heart, this tremble that tells her she will be, like her mother, forever afraid of being lonely.

Sometimes, even after twenty-six years, either Deb or I, at some ordinary moment – washing dishes, straightening closets, sweeping floors – will find ourselves overwhelmed with emotion, a rush of thanksgiving for all the time we've had together. One of us will rush to the other, and we'll wrap ourselves up in a fierce embrace. "One of those times," we call such moments, flashes of gratitude that rush into the heart and nearly knock us over with their force.

I'm sure that we feel these moments with such intensity because there was a time some years back when we almost walked away from each other, called an end to what before that time we had named "love." I'm convinced that what kept us from making the final break was the fact that, despite the difficulties we were suffering, we were each other's best friend, and there was something about that fact that remained indestructible no matter the ugly words and hurtful actions that we tried to levy against it. When we finally came out the other side of our trouble, we knew love in a way that we hadn't in those early years. We knew it as something forbearing and patient, willing to wait for us until we were truly capable of it.

A true love story is never separate from the others that have preceded it and the ones that will follow, never detached from the collective yearning, the collective fear that is our blessing and our curse from the moment we first draw breath and reach with our cry for someone to hold us, to touch us with tenderness, to let us know we aren't alone.

I can imagine Deb and I both mulling over the story of Mary Ann, dreaming it as we move through our days. Perhaps on occasion we even dream it at the same time. Maybe, during the silence of an evening, when we glance up from our reading and catch each other's eye, we're imagining the moment I've yet to write, the one where Clarissa leans close to Henry and whispers in his ear, tells him that Mary Ann would be tickled if he would buy her cake. "Nothing fancy," she says. "It's just a pound cake. The box has dried asters on it. You sure would make her day. She's sweet on you."

Of course, he's always known it to be true – of course he has. And he'll buy that cake – that pound cake – choke it down, because on this day, his last day for some time on Lukin Prairie, he wants to be in the company of someone like Mary Ann, someone who knows what it is to lose a father. He sits with her on the grass, after the bidding is done, and thinks about how, come nightfall, he'll sneak away – his father be damned – and go off to fight the war. He knows this in his heart and can't say it to anyone, not to his mother or Clarissa or his sister Sally, not to Benton or Alfred or William Bell.

Then Mary Ann says, "You'd of done better with Annie's cake. It's chiffon. Just look at Uncle Benton over there. Ain't he a sight?"

Benton, who bid on Annie's cake when it was plain that Henry wouldn't, is sitting cross-legged on the ground, taking dainty bites.

Annie is sitting beside him, looking glum. He spears each little piece of cake with his fork and holds it up to the sunlight, twirling it on the fork's tines, squinting at it, as if it were a precious gem. Let him stay here, Henry thinks. Let him stay at home and eat fancy cakes. Henry holds a wedge of pound cake in his hands. He bites off a mouthful, imagining already the taste and weight of hardtack.

"Pound cake suits me fine," he says, not caring that crumbs are tumbling from his mouth, sticking to his chin, falling to his shirt front.

Mary Ann takes the handkerchief she has folded into the pocket of her dress and gently wipes the cake crumbs from Henry's face. She's careful not to let the raised stitches of the embroidery scratch him. He sticks out his chin just the slightest bit so she can clean it. Suddenly she's overcome by how he gives himself over to her as if they've been married for years.

Something about this intimacy strikes Henry, too, and before he knows it, he's telling her his secret. "I'm going off tonight," he says. "Going off to Lancaster to join up."

Mary Ann's heart races. "Your daddy," she says.

"He won't know," says Henry. "Not 'til it's too late."

Mary Ann looks out across the grove to the couples who are lazing now. Some of the men have lain back on the grass, their hands behind their heads. The women sit demurely, their legs tucked under them, hidden beneath the swirls of their skirts. Henry's mother and father are there, and Alfred and Sally, and Clarissa and William, and Grandpa and Grandma Ridgley. The wheat has been threshed, the hay is almost in. Everyone is alive and well and thankful for this splendid day. A lone crow calls from overhead, but not even that screech can disturb the men and women at rest in the grove. Even Annie has started to giggle. Something Benton has said has tickled her.

"I won't tell anyone," Mary Ann says.

And that's when Henry knows. He knows that whatever lies ahead of him, he'll play this moment over and over in his head: he and Mary Ann in the shade, sealing secrets, while the leaves shiver above them. He doesn't dare say, or even think, the word "love," nor does she. But that's what's blossoming inside them, unfolding as delicately as the pink-tinged petals of blackberry blooms, tickling their chests, their throats, their tongues.

They have no idea that over a hundred years later, I'll try to imagine their story – my great-grandparents – a story that begins the day Jonathan Inyart dies and leaves Clarissa a widow and Mary Ann to grow to be this girl who can promise herself to Henry Martin with that simple vow, "I won't tell."

The crow calls once more and then wheels off across the sky. Mary Ann closes her eyes and listens to the voices in the grove. How low they are, how far away they seem. She wonders how long it will be before she sees Henry again. She won't even allow herself to think that he might die in the war. He doesn't speak, but she knows he's there. She can hear his breathing, can feel ever so lightly against her arm the tickle of his shirt sleeve. She thinks of her father's fiddle and how, if he were still alive, he would play it at her wedding. She remembers the chant from the hayfield: "One I love, two I love, three I love, I say." She'll count to four, and there he'll be – Henry Martin – hers now, at least for this afternoon, for this glorious, glorious day.

I have seen only that one photograph of them, the one taken late in their lives, sitting side by side in chairs on a wooden walkway outside their house. They look so old, it seems impossible that they could have once been young, but they were.

Imagine them in the grove, content to let the afternoon lengthen, and the sun dip below the tree line, and the light dim until they must rise, as do the others, everyone moving now toward home, toward the night of rest and dream and, if God wills, the morrow. Another day, and all it brings.

Leave them to whatever secrets of the heart they protected through the years. Leave them, moving through the dark, not speaking, enchanted and terrified, staring into what has just become the rest of their lives.

5
Turning Bones

I imagine my grandmother on the last day of her girlhood, the day my grandfather comes to say his wife, Ella, is dying from tuberculosis. This is in 1901, and my grandmother, Stella, is eighteen years old. Ella is twenty-six, married ten years to Will Martin, mother of two children: Glen, age nine, and Mae, age five.

Stella Inyart lives a half-mile to the east atop a hill that gently slopes to the fields below. Will Martin has to cross one of those fields when he finally comes to the Inyarts, asking for help. Perhaps Stella sees him as he steps carefully over the corn rows, plants ankle-high. Perhaps she takes note of his narrow shoulders, the way he leans forward as he climbs the hill, his head down, ever mindful as he is of the young corn plants. And maybe this is the moment when her heart goes out to him, when he becomes someone she can love.

Already, her sisters have married: Ida and Laura and Della and Nellie and Fannie. And here she is still living at home. "Near 'bout ripe," her father often teases her. Sometimes she stands a good while studying her face in the looking glass. Her nose is too flat – not daintily tipped like Laura's, and her hair is short and coarse, kept in tight pin curls. How she's always envied Ida's black mane and the way it ripples and gleams when she brushes it. Still, for the most part, Stella thinks herself pleasing. She has full lips, a dimple in her chin, a slim figure, and a grace when she takes a turn at a barn dance. People are always remarking on how willowy she is. Years later, at my father's funeral, a third cousin will take my hand and say, "You put me in mind of Stella. Just the way you walk across the room."

By the time I know my grandmother, over fifty years will have passed since the day Will Martin stepped over the last of the corn rows and into her yard. She'll be nearly blind with cataracts, but still tall, still graceful, her fingers long and narrow. Though she can barely see, she'll cut rags into strips, wind those strips into balls, and then weave multicolored rugs, creating something pretty from scraps she's been able to salvage.

It's easy for me, then, to imagine her and her mother sitting in the yard on ladder-back chairs that morning in 1901, stitching together reticules, the dainty drawstring purses women carried in those days. I can see my grandmother doing needlepoint on the face of the broadcloth, embroidering the blue petals of forget-me-nots, trailing the curls of their tendrils with green thread.

She doesn't even look up when Will Martin says, "It's Ella. She's bad sick with the consumption."

"I'll come look after her," Stella says. She knows how contagious the disease is, but she doesn't hesitate. "I'll see to your young'uns, too. I'll be there this noon," she says. Then she bites off the thread with her teeth.

On the island of Madagascar people believe that their dead ancestors have the power to bestow fortune or tragedy on the surviving family. The stone and cement tombs are often in better condition than the clay houses of the living. From May to November, the winter months of Madagascar, people pull the remains of loved ones from their tombs and dance with the corpses in a ceremony known as *famadi-hana*, which literally means "turning of bones."

In my home, when I was a child, there was never dancing, and rarely music. On the farm where I lived with my parents and my grandmother, Stella, there was no piano, no music box, no phonograph. Occasionally my father would try to sing a verse of a song – "Rescue the Perishing" or "Daisy" – in an off-key voice. From time to time, at the end of the mutual-news broadcast on the radio, a few bars of dance music would sneak into our house. Saturday nights we watched *The Lawrence Welk Show* on television; we sat in dim light, the glow from the television screen flickering over our faces. We sat there, rarely speaking, as nimble girls twirled and hale men broke into song. We sang in church, but that was a joyless type of singing, with no music to accompany it, since the Church of Christ believed the use of musical instruments during worship services to be a sin. The song leader called out the hymns in a monotone. Plain voices measured out the time of each verse. If we intended to make "a joyful noise," we failed miserably. We went about our worship with a severity learned from the grim forbearance it took to perform farm work. We were, for the most part, quiet and reserved.

We were particularly shy about our dead. Because my family rarely spoke of him, I knew little about my grandfather, Will. I knew nothing of Ella at all. I knew my father had a half brother and a half sister, but I didn't really understand what that meant, and I must admit that I wasn't curious the way I am now, when I am the last of the Martin family, forced to imagine my ancestors from the few clues photographs offer and the public records I find in courthouses. Then it was as if we had put the dead away from us and didn't mean to disturb them. Their photographs were kept in boxes in my grandmother's wardrobe, the same photographs I now pull out again and again. I study the way my ancestors face the camera head-on, not smiling. They look timid, helpless, as if they know they have nothing more to offer than their modest looks, their homespun clothes. They can't say this, but they look as if they're desperate for someone to get beyond their grim visages to the lives they carry inside them, to finally, please, tell their stories.

Is it love or fear or both that impels the people on Madagascar toward such an urgent recovery of the dead? It would be easy to consider this dancing with corpses a gruesome thing, but isn't it also a profound passion, an ardent desire for reunion? For months after my father's death in 1982, he came to me in dreams. I found him sitting in chairs, standing on sidewalks. "You're supposed to be dead," I would tell him, and at the sound of my voice he would start to fall, to crumple like a scarecrow released from his post. I would grab him, hold him to me, stagger about with his weight, knowing that eventually I would have to let him go, but not for a while, not yet, not while I could feel him against my skin.

My family's dead have crept inside me. I've poked around in courthouse records; handled brittle documents; studied my ancestors' signatures or marks on marriage licenses, land deeds, probate records; seen their names recorded on certificates of birth and death. Their souls have transmigrated through the generations, leaving one body for another, gathering, finally, in my own, a chain of spirits as impossible to escape as the double helix of DNA. The dead surrender to the drift of time. They dance about, all essence now – energy and force – waiting for the living to find them, to take them inside as easily as one would take a breath.

Deb refuses to speak of the time she feared I would die. It was January 1979, and I was sick with pneumonia, only no one knew it. An emergency room doctor had misdiagnosed my condition as an upper respiratory infection, given me an injection, and sent me home. Day by day I got sicker. Even now it's difficult for me to relive that time – the fevered dreams, the wracking coughs, the way the world had stopped seeming real to me. On the rare occasions when I slept, it must have been easy for Deb to imagine me a corpse – pale and still – to imagine that both my body and my soul had surrendered.

I don't know how sick Ella was the day Stella came to care for her, but by then the tubercle bacilli would have multiplied in the small air sacs of the lungs. I can imagine how they must have choked and suffocated her. I suspect she was coughing when Stella stepped into the log house; I can see her spitting clots of sputum and blood into a rag, a scrap torn from an old flour sack.

Stella takes the rag from her, finds a clean one, and soaks it in cool water. She bathes Ella's face – Ella who lies on the corn-shuck mattress in the log house, deep in a grove of oak trees.

"It's the consumption," she says. Her lips are dry and cracked. Sweat glistens along her collarbone, gathers in the hollow of her throat.

"I know it is," Stella says. She holds a dipper of water to Ella's lips and lifts her head so she can drink. "Don't worry. I'm here to see to you."

We can trace the presence of mycobacterium tuberculosis back to 2400 B.C. Fragments of the spinal columns from Egyptian mummies show pathological signs of tubercular decay. The disease, up until 1944, when the antibiotic streptomycin proved to be successful, was humanity's most dreaded enemy – so deadly that even Hippocrates, well-known for his honorable code of medical ethics, warned his colleagues around 460 B.C. against visiting tubercular patients in the late stages of their illness because the inevitable deaths might mar the doctors' reputations.

A succession of effective drugs followed the introduction of strep-

tomycin: p-aminosalicylic acid (1949), isoniazid (1952), pyrazina-
mide (1954), cycloserine (1955), ethambutol (1962), and rifampicin
(1963). From 1953 to 1984, thanks to these drugs, the number of tuberculosis cases reported in the United States decreased by an aver-
age of 6 percent each year. Since 1985, due in part to the HIV epidemic
and increased migration from countries where tuberculosis is common, the number of cases has increased. Still, the disease isn't the
feared killer that it was before the advent of chemotherapy treat-
ment. At the time of Ella's illness, particularly in the rural areas,
where healthcare was often distant and unaffordable, there was little
to be done outside the usual folk remedies (a tea and poultice from
the lungwort plant, for example) or superstitious charms (such as a
ball of the fetid resin from the asafoetida plant worn on a string tied
around the neck). The people like my ancestors who settled southern
Illinois died of cholera, influenza, summer complaint, tuberculosis.
Given the hard labor of clearing woodlands for farming, the coaxing
of seed to plant and grain, the fear of Indian attacks, and the brutal
isolation of winter's cold and snow, dying was perhaps one of the
easiest things one could accomplish.

When I was ill with pneumonia, I never once thought that I would
die. In fact, I thought each day that I would take a turn toward the
better and start to improve. When I didn't – when it became clear
that I was in trouble – I finally said to Deb, who all along had wanted
me to go back to the doctor, "All right. Take me." And she did. I was
twenty-three at the time, only a few years younger than Ella when
she lay dying of tuberculosis. She must have known her days were
dwindling, because at some point during her illness she put in writing her wish that her son, Glen, and her daughter, Mae, each receive
eighteen dollars and fifty cents after her death. I know this to be true
because I've seen the probate record filed in 1906, five years after
Ella's death, testifying that the money had been delivered to the
rightful heirs. My grandfather's signature is on the document, as is
my great-grandfather's mark as witness.

I wasn't present at either of my parents' deaths, and this is a fact
that causes me both grief and thanksgiving. I'm not sure that I would
have been up to the task; I regret that I never had the chance. What
must it be like to watch a loved one die? I don't know, but I imagine
it must split you in two: one part hoping for a miracle, another anx-

ious for the suffering to be done. Circumstance and distance protected me from this agony. My father died suddenly from a heart
attack while mowing the grass in the summer heat; my mother died
a more difficult death in a nursing home some four hundred miles
from where I lived at the time. In a way I'm glad I was spared from
having to see either death, but at the same time I feel diminished
somewhat because I wasn't there to do whatever would have been
required of me: to lay my hand to cheek or brow, to offer whatever I
could to ease the soul's passage from the world.

In the latter half of the nineteenth century and the early part of
the twentieth, farm families, when they traveled in search of better
land, did so together. In the case of my ancestors, the Martins traveled with the Fites. More than once, through the generations, Martins and Fites married, owned land in the same townships, attended
to one another's births and deaths. Why then, in 1901, wasn't it a Fite
who cared for Ella? Or why wasn't it Will Martin's sister-in-law,
Clara? Henry Fite owned eighty acres just north of Will Martin's
forty; Charlie Martin, Will's brother, owned forty acres to the south.

But Will turns to Stella Inyart, possibly because his own mother
was an Inyart, or possibly because he's already noted Stella's goodness, has perhaps begun to fancy her. Maybe the Inyarts are known
as healers. I remember my grandmother, in her old age, believing in
the powers of herbs: horehound, sassafras, castor oil. And her
daughter, my aunt, nursing her son through seizures, fevers, infections of the colon and kidneys and bladder. I remember my father's
first cousin Raymond Inyart, digging ginseng root from the woods
of Lukin Township. Maybe Will hopes that Stella will come into the
log house and find a way to save Ella, but, of course, she can't. It's
1901 in rural southern Illinois, and when someone becomes ill with
consumption, they die. There's nothing Stella can do, but she goes,
putting her own health at risk. Maybe she does it because she sees
Will ragged with worry and takes pity on him and his two children,
who are so sweet-faced, their features delicate like their mother's.
Maybe it's Stella's nature; I know it's what I learned from my own
father, who must have learned it from his parents: when a neighbor
needs help, you give it.

My grandmother, when I was five, was already seventy-seven. She
was an old woman in poor health, impatient with a boy like me, who

was often noisy and rambunctious. Everything about her was so severe: the crinkled pins she used to hold her hair in a bun, the dark
support hose she wore, the sunbonnet that cowled her face when she
went outside, the brown bread she ate, the All-Bran cereal, the Black
Drought laxative powders she took. For the most part, I found her to
be a stifling, joyless presence in our house. I had yet to understand
how physical debilitation – my grandmother's cataracts, in this case,
her heart disease and arthritis – not only wracks the body but also
alters the personality. How can the essence of a person sustain itself
when the vessel that houses it begins to break down?

Often, during the few years my grandmother lived in our house,
she lay in bed – "too puny," she said, to get up. In those days doctors
in our part of the country still made house calls. Doc Stoll came
regularly to see my grandmother. I was fascinated with the black
satchel he carried, the one that opened like a valise, and the stethoscope he wore around his fat neck. One day, as he examined my
grandmother, I peeked around the doorjamb and saw her sitting up
in bed, her nightgown undone, Doc Stoll's stethoscope between her
naked breasts. I had, of course, never seen my grandmother's breasts,
and I was, at once, embarrassed and entranced – not from any erotic
instinct (at least, none that I was conscious of) but because the skin I
was seeing, in comparison to the wrinkled and age-spotted flesh of
her face, was so smooth and white. So young. So like my own.

At that moment my grandmother became more real to me, more
complete. Her life, I sensed, stretched back through years and moments I was incapable of imagining. That afternoon I got into bed
with her, and she put her arm around me, and in a soft voice she told
me stories about my father when he was a boy. I remember the feel of
the quilt over me, the way the ticking of the feather pillows smelled.
It was raining outside, and as the afternoon went on the light grew
dim in the room, and finally I slept, curled in close to my grandmother, who once, long ago, had been kind to a woman who was
dying, a woman whose death made my own life possible.

When does Will Martin know that Ella is nearly lost to him? Maybe
it's a day when he's outside scattering feed for his chickens, and he
hears Stella in the house, singing to Glen and Mae. She's singing
"They're Gathering Homeward," and her voice is so sweet, Will starts

to cry. Or maybe it's an evening when Stella sits by Ella's bed and shows her the reticule she's made. "I've brought it for you," she says, and Ella, in a weak, gasping voice, says, "Oh, I won't be needing that."

But Stella insists. She fetches Ella's worn reticule from the wardrobe and transfers objects to the new one, the one embroidered with forget-me-nots. Will watches her handle Ella's leather coin purse, an old penny stick of peppermint candy, a handkerchief, a mother-of-pearl button that fell from her dress on one of the last days that she was well.

They had made the ten-mile trip into Sumner to get their portrait made at Ronald's Studio. Will wore a suit and necktie. He fastened only the top button of his coat, as was the fashion of the day. Ella wore a long, dark dress, the pleated frill of a jabot rippling down the front to the belted waist. She had dressed the children: Mae in a white shift with ruffles at the collar and the cuffs of the sleeves; Glen in a double-breasted suit with a white cavalier collar, trimmed with lace, falling over the shoulders, a watch dangling from a fob stretched from pocket to buttonhole.

I have the photo now. Will sits on a ladder-back chair, his hands on the tops of his legs. Glen, to his right, and Mae, to his left, rest their small hands on him. Ella is behind him and to his left, her hand on his shoulder. It's as if the three of them are consoling him, bracing him for the sadness that's soon to come.

I've made the button fall from Ella's dress, a pure act of imagination, because if the button falls there in the photographer's studio and Will retrieves it and presses it into Ella's hand, they come alive for me. They step from the frame of the camera's lens and begin to move – my grandfather and his wife, who must feel so handsome in their best clothes, so proud of their darling children, that the dropped button is only an inconvenience, something Ella will sew back on her dress quick as she can.

But here it is again, the button still in her reticule, fished out by Stella, and when Will sees it, he nearly breaks down, the sight of that pearl button too much for him, thinking, as he is, that it wasn't so long ago that Ella took it from him, and neither of them knew that their time together was nearly gone.

"It's funny, isn't it?" Stella says to Ella. "You and me having nearly the same name."

"Phoebe," Ella says. "My real name is Phoebe."

Will thinks of morning light, and birds singing, and how fresh the world once seemed to him each day when he first opened his eyes.

She was sixteen when he married her – Phoebe Ellen Preston, a slim-waisted girl, her hair curled and piled on top of her head. They were married on May 30 by a justice of the peace. Ella's mother, Elizabeth, certified that she approved the marriage; my great-grandfather, Henry, scratched an X where the county clerk instructed him, signifying that he accepted Elizabeth's consent as genuine.

I can imagine Will and Ella, there at the beginning of their married life. Ella, if the photograph I have of her from this time is a fair indication, is timid, a bit cowed by how fast her life is changing. Married – my word. And Will, only twenty-two, is young enough to marvel over the fact that whatever happens from then on will be linked to this girl who is now his wife.

Surely, there's a shivaree that night. Neighbors and relatives from Lukin Township sneak down the lane to Will and Ella's house after they've gone to bed, and there in the dark they strike up a din by firing shotguns into the air, banging on washtubs, ringing cowbells, blowing on horns. And Will, as is the custom, steps outside in his nightshirt and offers everyone apples and coffee and crullers. Perhaps there's even a jug of corn liquor that the men pass around in the shadows. And then the fiddles come out and the Jew's harps and the squeezeboxes, and all night, by the light of pine-knot torches, Will and Ella dance. He puts his hand lightly on her slender waist and twirls her about in a glorious reel. She tosses back her head and sees the stars shining through the canopy of trees, and maybe she thinks she's never been as happy as she is now and wishes that the music and the dancing and the feel of her husband's hand on her waist could go on and on.

Now in the log house, as night deepens, the only sounds are the rasp of Ella's breathing, the squeak of Stella's rocking chair, the gentle click of her knitting needles. She sits near the hearth, relying on the light of the fire to see. Will, who has put Glen and Mae to bed in the loft, stands at the bottom of the ladder and looks beyond Ella's bed to Stella by the fire. In the shadows she can be anyone he chooses. She can be Ella, young and healthy. He has to fight an impulse rising in him, one he hates himself for having – a desire to go to Stella, to kneel at her feet and lay his head in her lap as if he were no older than Glen or little Mae. He wants to feel Stella's hand stroking his face, the way it does Ella's after she's changed her nightdress or braided her hair. He's gone beyond worry into the first dark days of grief, and now that he's convinced that Ella will die, he wants nothing more than for someone to comfort him – for Stella to comfort him. So kind she's been to Ella, to Glen and Mae – so gentle – he hasn't been able to stop himself, though he doesn't know this yet, from falling in love with her. He only knows this nearly irrepressible urge to be near her, an urge he covers over with gruffness.

"You ought to go on now and sleep," he says to her.

She doesn't lift her head from her knitting. "Not tonight," she says in a hushed voice. "Tonight I mean to keep awake."

Will knows that she's telling him that tonight may be Ella's last. He marks it in his mind – July 22, 1901. He doesn't know that in a little more than a year, he and Stella will marry, will live together in this log house where he and Ella first lay down as husband and wife. He doesn't know how, at the same time, he will love and resent Stella, feel himself simultaneously drawn toward her goodness and repelled by her association with Ella's dying.

In the years prior to 1882, when Robert Koch discovered that a bacterium caused tuberculosis, some people believed that the ailment was the result of vampires feeding on the living. The patients gradually wasted away even though they had an increased hunger. After they died, their relatives often got sick, presumably because the vampires knew where to find them. To put a stop to this feeding, people began to disinter the bodies of their dead relatives – to burn the heart or to place the skull on the chest with the leg bones crossed below it, believing that these drastic measures would kill the vampire.

Will Martin will never be able to rid himself of the haunting sensation that he has somehow caused Ella's illness. He took her into town, let the photographer make their picture, and something in the powder flash crept into her lungs and began to destroy her. Fantastic, I know, but this is the way of my family – this capacity for self-blame. Whatever goes wrong is somehow the fault of our own flaws. We look for causes, culpability, refusing to accept the fact that sometimes chance and circumstances collide. Someone coughs – it may have happened anywhere – and Ella breathes in a tubercular bacterium, and at that moment, in 1901, everything is determined. I can't change that aspect of the story; all I can do is speculate on these last days when Ella and Will and Stella are inextricably linked, then and forever.

Perhaps, on this last night, Ella rallies for a moment. Maybe she sits up in bed and says, "I'm just about starved to death."

In the milk house, kept cool by the double walls lined with sawdust, there are pieces left from the chicken Stella fried for their supper. She has wrapped a drumstick, a wishbone, a wing in cloth and closed them up in a tin pail. When she goes to fetch it, she carries an oil lamp. Despite the heat it throws up into her face, she shivers inside the milk house. She remembers how Will looked at her the morning he came to say Ella was sick – like he was lost. She knew then that she could have whatever she wanted from him. She understands now – and this strikes her with such force she feels faint – that the rest of her life is about to begin. Ella will die, and she – Stella – will marry Will, and no longer will she have to abide her father's teasing or look with envy at her sister's long, black hair. She doesn't know yet how some people will gossip, talk about what must have been going on in that house between her and Will Martin – and his wife dying from consumption.

But it hasn't been that way at all. They've rarely even spoken, and then only to say the necessary things – to talk of food and chores and Ella and the children. Stella has slept on a pallet by Ella's bed. She has risen time and time again in the night to fetch Ella water, to help her to the chamber pot. She has washed her fevered body, has cooked whatever foods Ella has requested. Her appetite seems boundless. And there have been the children to see to, and Will – his clothes to mend, his spirits to try to maintain.

Just the other day, when she went out to the cistern, she found a robin's egg. It was so small, no bigger than the end of her thumb, and colored such a pale blue. She put it on Will's plate, and when he came to breakfast, she said, "Looks like the hens are getting uppity." And he laughed: a loud, sudden bark – Ha! – and then silence.

Now she feels guilty about causing that laugh, letting that brief moment of joy into the house. She wonders whether she did it –

whether she has done everything for Ella and Will and their two young'uns – not from goodness alone, but also from want. If this is true, she refuses to feel ashamed. She understands that at the heart of everything – even death – beats the desire to love and to be loved in return.

I have inherited my grandmother's photographs and mementos. Included in them is the portrait Will and Ella had made just before she fell ill. There is also the one of Ella as a young girl, and another of her and Will and Glen as a baby. Nowhere is there a photograph of Will and Stella together, and something about that fact suggests to me an emptiness through all their years together. After Ella died, was it too painful for him to ever again step into a photographer's studio? How much joy went out of him when Ella died? More than his marriage to my grandmother could ever refill?

Deb and I married because I was about to leave for college, and we couldn't bear the thought of being apart. I don't know whether that's what love is – this urgent longing for someone's presence – but our original impetus for marriage has sustained us now nearly twenty-seven years, has seen us through some perilous times. No matter how tenuous our relationship has become, an elemental truth has always existed: neither of us has been able to imagine a life apart from the other. Perhaps this is what frightened Deb most of all the winter she feared that I might die – the notion of the space my leaving would create, the thought of my spirit a wave somewhere in the universe, undulating around her, a presence she would sense but never be able to touch.

I suspect that when you attend to someone's death, as Stella did Ella's, you bind yourself to that person forever. Some part of them goes inside you, and even if you want to expel it, you can't.

Perhaps on this night, when she stands in the milk house, Stella realizes that her true intimacy has been with Ella – that this is what she and Will are going to share, are going to look for in each other all the thirty-nine years they will be married: the memory of Ella and how, when she finally slipped away, she filled them forever.

When Stella comes in from the milk house, she sets the oil lamp on the table beside Ella's bed, and there in its glow she opens the tin pail and unwraps the chicken. She watches as Ella's teeth tear at skin and meat. She licks her fingers; her chin is shiny with grease. She eats the drumstick, and the wing, and finally the wishbone. Stella takes the bones from her, holds them in her palm, aware that from across the room Will is watching her, that above them Glen and Mae have awakened and crept to the edge of the loft, where they kneel and look down on their mother.

"Do the wishbone with me," Ella says. She takes one of the sides, and Stella takes the other. When she pulls, she feels little resistance from Ella. The wishbone snaps, and Stella is left holding the longer fragment. Ella holds a splinter of bone on her palm, holds it up to the light from the oil lamp. "Just a little hank of bone," she says. "That's all I could manage. Sakes alive, it looks like you get your wish."

The splintered bone is nearly transparent in the light. Such an airy, insubstantial thing, Stella thinks. She's aware of Will moving toward the bed, his footsteps shaking the floor planks. He starts to take the bone from Ella, but before he can grab onto it, it slips from her hand, tumbles down to the floor, where a gust of wind catches it and sends it skittering off into the dark shadows at the corner of the room.

Will starts to go after it, but Ella grabs his hand. "We'll find it come morning," she says. "Don't fret about it now."

Will reaches out his other hand for Stella, but she can't take it because both her hands are holding the chicken bones, and she's afraid that, if she tries to put them in one hand, she'll end up dropping them all. She can't bear the thought that this might be the last sound Ella hears, the clacking dance of the bones as they fall.

6
Fire Season

Maybe it was cholera, ague, typhoid, influenza. Or it could have been dropsy, nephritis, apoplexy, consumption. It might have been grief over the death of her daughter Nancy. All I know is that for some reason lost now, my great-great-grandmother, Elizabeth Gaunce Martin, died in the autumn of 1866, and her husband of those thirty-three years – John, who had taken her to Ohio and on to Indiana and finally to Illinois – was suddenly without her.

At the Brian Cemetery, on the day of Elizabeth's burial, the hickory trees would have been yellow; the nuts, their black husks splitting, would have lain in the brown grass. I imagine John's boots, freshly blacked, shuffling through that grass, his steps weary and halting, as he makes his way down the hill from the graveyard. His children are with him: William and Sarah, grown now, and the ones still at home – Henry, back from the war, George, Jackson, Robert, Louisa.

Louisa pauses at the graveyard's gate and looks back toward the hickories. "Aren't the trees pretty?" she says, and John hears the grief hidden beneath her bright voice.

Although he's not ordinarily an affectionate man around his children, he puts his arm around Louisa's shoulder – too roughly, he fears, because he knocks her straw hat, the one Sarah pinned to her hair, askew. Louisa stands there, the hat tilted to the side, a silly look on her face, and she says, "Oh, Pa."

He straightens the hat for her, knowing that she's the one he feels most sorry for, the one who will miss her mother most. Prudence Louisa, named after Lizzie's sister, a name that now seems a mistake, since Louisa is anything but prudent. She's irrational, indecisive. A mooncalf, Henry sometimes says. A twitterbug, chattering and giggling and buzzing about like a honeybee crazy for clover. She's always relied on Lizzie to steady her, even after becoming a grown woman. "Mommy, what dress will I wear?" "Mommy, I can't tie my sash." "Oh, Mommy."

John knows, this day as they leave the graveyard, that Louisa will never marry. He's sure that his other children will find their way in the world – have started to already – but Louisa, oh, his sweet, silly Louisa, she will always be his baby girl, too simple, too useless to be someone's wife.

"Yes, the trees are pretty, Lou," he says. "Now let's go on. Let's go home."

"Home?" she says, a crestfallen look on her face, and he knows she'll be completely lost without Lizzie.

"Yes, home," he says.

He herds her down the stone steps cut into the hill, feeling, in a way he never has, his duty toward his daughter.

At bedtime she comes to him in her sleeping gown, her hair un- done, a wild bramble, a brush held in her hand. "Mommy always brushed my hair." She reaches out the brush to him. "Every night," she says.

He's sitting in a rocker by the window, letting the night air rush in, warm enough here at Indian summer to please him. It carries the scent of wood smoke and leaf must and the sounds of cornstalks, their dry blades scraping together. If it were a normal night – if Lizzie were still alive – she would join him here, and they would sit awhile, thankful for the harvest – corn and tobacco and pumpkins – and for Henry come home to them from the war, for Sarah and her good husband, Alfred Ridgley, and William, a grown man now, earning his own wage as James French's live-in hired man. John and Elizabeth would give thanks for all they had survived: the cholera that had al- most taken him before they could marry, the birthings that she had managed, the journey they had made from Kentucky to Ohio, and the drought that had driven them west, thirsting for rain. They had lost Nancy, but still, compared to other families who had buried child after child, they had been blessed.

"Can't you manage your hair tonight?" John says. He knows that if he touches Louisa's hair, he'll remember what it felt like a long time ago when Lizzie's pigtails brushed across his arm.

Louisa makes a few clumsy swipes of the brush. "It's all tangled up," she says. "Mommy always said the cats must have been sucking on it."

"Come here, then," he says.

And Louisa kneels at the window, her back to him. He drags the brush gently through her hair, glossy in the moonlight. He thinks of Lizzie with the angels in Heaven.

"A hundred strokes," Louisa says. Her head tips back slightly at the brush's tug. "That's what Mommy always did."

John feels something awakening in him, a tenderness the years and years of farm work have stolen from him. How odd, he thinks, here at the time of Lizzie's death, that he should find himself returned to love.

"All right," he says. "A hundred." He counts the strokes softly with the slightest whisper of breath, imagines Lizzie counting with him, the two of them brushing their daughter's hair.

It's hard for me to write of death these days. One of my oldest and dearest friends is fighting for his life. He lies in a burn unit at Loyola University Medical Center near Chicago, while far away, in Texas, I wait for news. One week ago, at 1:45 in the morning, my friend's house exploded. Brad was alone in the house, sleeping in his bedroom on the second floor, which at the moment of the blast ceased to exist, the house reduced to rubble, engulfed in flames.

It's only occasionally, in the privacy of my mind, that I can work up the courage to imagine the details. I won't evoke them here. Let me say the words: *gas leak, explosion, fire.* You can imagine the rest.

And I think it's important to practice this empathy, to imagine the sequence of events, to feel as much as is possible the horror Brad woke to, to imagine myself in his place. It's the step we don't take when tragedy's victim is a stranger to us. But when the face on the news, the name in the paper, belongs to someone we love, how can we help ourselves? For what we learn at these times is how deeply and richly we're connected. So I make the journey out of love, out of some hope that Brad's spirit, whether it rests now in some calm dream or twists in frenzy and chaos, will know that there are people who would have it come back to them.

*

John, after Lizzie's death, keeps waiting for his life to feel familiar to him. He wants to wake in the morning and not have the terrible ache in his chest, the realization that he faces another day without his dear Lizzie.

Indian summer fades, and the cold winds of November sweep across the prairie. They strip the last of the leaves from their branches, and when John goes to the graveyard, the hickories are bare.

He and the boys make ready for winter. They butcher hogs and salt down the meat. They store fruits and vegetables in the root cellar: apples and turnips, potatoes and squashes, cabbages and dried beans. They build an ash hopper out by the cistern and cobble a roof over it to keep the ashes dry until soap-making time come spring.

John shows Louisa how to scrape ashes from the home fires and carry them out to the hopper. "You remember how Mommy did it?"

"Yes, I remember Mommy."

"Well, you're the mommy now."

Louisa giggles. "Oh, Pa."

"You are, Lou. You're the woman of the house. You're the one who has to keep things going."

He knows that he's blowing hot air, that his words, even as he speaks them, are flaming up and falling away to ash. Louisa can't ramrod this house. Through winter John and Jackson and George and Robert will all do their share. And Sarah will come by, when she can spare the time away from her own home, to lend a hand. But come spring, when it's time to plow and plant the fields, John and the boys will be on the run from daylight to dark, and he wonders how they'll manage then.

One Sunday, when Sarah and Alfred are there, John asks her to write a letter to his sister Malinda, in Indiana. Malinda Fite, for she married Joseph and left Ohio some twenty-seven years ago. The thought overwhelms John. Has it really been that long since he and Lizzie and his mother and father all lived with the Fites? Sarah was little more than a suckling then, and here she is all grown and a mother to a daughter of her own – Elizabeth, who is seven now, with hair as blond as Lizzie's when John first took note of her in Kentucky.

Sarah's hand is sure; the nib of her pen scratches across the paper. "Dearest sister," she writes. "It's news of no count I send you."

She sits at the long table in the kitchen. John paces back and forth behind her, telling her what to say. He says that Lizzie is dead, that Louisa is lost without her, that they are all managing tolerable here in winter, but that he dreads the spring and summer when he and the boys will be working all day in the fields and Louisa will be alone in the house. How will she have their meals ready for them? How will she clean and mend their clothes? "Sarah is a blessing," he says, "but so busy with a family of her own." He asks after Malinda and Joseph's children, the eight of them. The oldest girls are thirty and twenty-six, and like Louisa they still live at home, but they are able and full of their father's smarts and their mother's common sense. "You're so lucky to have Ursula and Matilda," he says. "I'm sure they ease your way."

Sarah lays down her pen and blots the ink dry. "Louisa can't help it she's simple," she says in a quiet voice that injures John. He hasn't meant to be hurtful, only to state the facts.

"Of course she can't," he says. "I didn't mean her any harm."

But he was sharp with her that morning in church when she began to giggle during the sermon and he clamped down on her wrist. "Louisa," he whispered. "You hush." He squeezed until she whimpered and then went mute.

He feels guilty now, and guilty still the next morning, when he carries a harness over to Ed Phillips's place to be mended. A hame has snapped in two, and one of the traces has torn and won't last another season.

Ed is out in his barnlot stacking barrel staves, layering them in crisscrosses so the air can move freely over each one – so sun, rain, wind, and frost can cure the wood before he cuts the staves and hollows them with his adz, joints them, and sets them into hoops that he stamps and punches and calls good.

John knows, because Ed has told him, that from the time he fells an oak tree to the time he uses the staves for barrels two winters will go by, the wood losing water little by little until it's cured enough to hold tight.

"I'll put your harness right as rain," he tells John. "Soon as I fire up my forge. You go on up to the house. Get in out of this mess. Eliza's still got the coffee hot."

Eliza is the third child of James and Elizabeth French – a tall, willowy girl, the same age as Louisa, but here she is – Eliza – already kneading dough for noontime biscuits. The breakfast dishes have been scrubbed and stacked. The floors have been swept. A pile of mending waits for her darning needles. And just as Ed has promised, a pot of coffee warms on the hearth.

"Oh, I can feel the cold on you," she says as she helps him off with his greatcoat. "Has it started to snow, Uncle Johnnie?"

"Starting to spit," he says. "Ed told me to come on up and get warm."

She's called him Uncle as long as he can remember – since the days when she played with his children and from time to time he gave them all a penny stick of candy.

"Sit down here by the fire," she says. "Let me pour you a cup."

The boy, Hosea, toddles over and places his hands on John's knees. The newborn, Laura, is sleeping in her cradle by the fire. It nearly breaks John's heart, the sweetness of these children on this bitter-cold day. How long it's been since his own were babes. The youngest, Robert, is now thirteen, growing into a man. John remembers one evening in Ohio, when he was at his grindstone, honing an ax blade, and Sarah and William came running to him to show off their cornhusk dolls. He set the ax aside and scooped them both up into his arms. He carried them into the house to Lizzie. "Aren't these the most handsome children you've ever seen?" John said, and when Lizzie answered her voice was shaking. "Oh, they are, John. They truly are."

And now she's gone, and his life is his, and the gravity of that thought – the notion that he is without a helpmeet, solitary now in the world – saddens him, and when he takes the cup from Eliza, he sees that his hands are trembling.

"You must be near froze," she says. He lets her cover his hands with her own and hold them steady. He feels the heat of the cup, the warmth of her skin. He tries to take a breath, but it catches in his throat, and when he tries to let it out, there's the noise of a choked sob, a cry that he's been carrying inside him since Lizzie died. It comes out now, and Eliza says, "You don't have to say a word. It's not for us to know the pain a body carries." He loves the soothing whisper of her voice. He knows she's speaking to him the way she does to her children when she wants to calm them. "Your heartache is yours.

I'd take it from you if I could. You just sit here now. Sit here as long as you want. I've always thought it peaceful by a fire. Just look at little Laura."

"I'm an old man," John says.

"No, you're not old," she tells him. "You're just put-upon right now."

The ancients trusted in fire. The Druids used it to divine the future. They studied the vertical shapes of smoke, its wisps and spirals, its puffs and trails. I'll admit to a similar fascination. I've always watched with wonder flames licking up from logs in the fireplace, or from candles, or from patio chimineas. What primal instinct is it that draws me so? I remember, as a child, begging my mother to let me light our fuel-oil stoves. She rolled a cone from newspaper for me, and as I held its narrow end, she struck a match and touched it to the flared cone. I stood still a moment, admiring my torch. "Light it quick," my mother said, and she guided my hand through the open hatch into the burner's drum. Together we swirled the cone around the drum's circumference. Fire blazed up with a whoosh. We pushed the newspaper inside, and I watched it blacken and curl and turn to ash, mesmerized by this vanishing act.

Now, since Brad's tragedy, I've fought to keep myself from thinking about the way skin burns, the way it is disfigured. That first evening, after Deb and I had received the mind-numbing news of the explosion, we both were careful not to mention the extent of Brad's injuries. We spoke with friends in Kentucky and Pennsylvania, friends who had managed to stay in touch since college days, who had made trips together over the years, stayed in one another's homes, remembered birthdays and anniversaries, were as close as family. Now one of us was in trouble; it was the first time this family of friends had been threatened with such a permanent and aching loss.

Finally our friends in Kentucky were able to get through to the hospital and speak to Brad's fiancée. The news wasn't good. Brad was burned over 80 percent of his body. The next seventy-two hours would be crucial. Deb and I held each other; we cried. Sorry, I can't beat back cliché here. We did what you do in real life when someone whom you love dearly might die.

That evening we watched the news report on WGN Chicago and saw amateur video of flames rising from the rubble of Brad's house high into the night sky. We sorted through details that we had gathered from this report and from newspaper articles we had retrieved from the Web. The fire chief said there had apparently been a gas leak inside the house but that he didn't yet know the ignition source. He said that Brad was "fairly severely burned" and that he had injuries to his arms – injuries that Brad's fiancée had described earlier as "deep lacerations." The man who lived in the duplex next to Brad's house said he had smelled gas a few months back, after the gas company installed a new meter. The gas company had to return to repair a loose pipe. The neighbor said he had smelled gas again a short time later, but when the gas company returned they said they didn't find any problem. Another neighbor reported that he had walked past Brad's house at seven P.M. and had smelled "a whiff" of gas. The neighbor's wife claimed that she had been smelling sewer gas the past few days and that at nine P.M. on the evening before the early-morning explosion it had been "really strong." Finally the *Chicago Tribune* reported that Brad had been conscious when firefighters pulled him from the rubble and that he had told them that he had smelled gas in his home that night and hadn't reported it.

Why in the world, Deb and I asked each other, hadn't anyone picked up the phone and called the gas company and stopped this horrible, horrible thing from happening? If I could practice pyromancy, I would divine the answer in fire.

Come spring, John covers his tobacco seedbeds with brush and sets it to burn. In this way he kills weed seeds and insects and hastens the warming of the soil. The dry brush crackles as it catches fire, and soon the heat is so fierce John and the boys have to back away into the shade of the deeper woods, where the Mayapples are growing up from the rot of last fall's dead leaves.

John watches the shimmery waves of heat wrinkling around the fire. It's been a winter now since Lizzie's death. It amazes him that he has made it through this season of days, through the gray skies and the short light, and come out here on this fine spring morning with so much left in the world that pleases him: the babble of creek water in the dark woods, the ringing of a woodpecker, the bright green of the Mayapples' broad leaves, the way Jackson and Robert and George squat down, their weight on the balls of their feet, as if at any instant they might spring up like deer. John squats down, too, feeling the strain in his knees, a stretching of tendon that tells him he's still flesh and bone and not wasted away by grief, as he imagined the day he sat in Eliza Phillips's house and felt as small as a tobacco seed, as puny. The wind, he thinks, could have lifted him and carried him away. That's how gone-to-nothing he was. But here he is now, another birthday gone. Fifty-seven he is, and amazed, but also saddened, that without Lizzie, he can still feel joy.

He imagines the charred ground after the brush has burned to ash. He and the boys will hoe the plot and rake the dirt and ash to a fine tilth before sowing the tobacco seed. They'll tamp the ground with the flat sides of their hoes, and by May, after morel mushrooms have popped up among the Mayapples, and the Mayapples themselves have bloomed and set fruit, the tobacco starts will be ready to transplant. Another crop begun. Another season of growing.

"Where's Henry this morning?" Jackson asks.

"He's helping out over to the Ridgleys," George says.

John listens with pleasure to their strong, clear voices ringing out in the quiet woods.

"Sweetening up Mary Ann is more like it," says Jackson.

"She's a honeybee," says Robert. "Henry better look out or he'll get stung."

Robert makes a buzzing sound and corkscrews his fingertip into Jackson's ribs. He does the same to George. Soon the boys are shoving at one another and wrestling around in the Mayapples.

As much as John enjoys the show, he can't bear the thought of those Mayapples crushed or, worse yet, wallowed up by their roots. He claps his hands together twice, and the sound is sharp enough to catch the boys' attention and bring their horseplay to a halt. Again John can hear the creek running, and the woodpecker, and the crackle of the fire.

"You leave Henry's business to Henry," he says. "Don't you know it's a sin to begrudge a man love?"

"Henry's in love." Robert, who hasn't completely shed his boyishness, giggles and squeals.

"Robert," John says with heat. "You hush."

John thinks he could sit here forever in the lush woods with his boys. But then he sees through the flames of the brush fire Louisa, her hair unpinned, her chest heaving. "Pa, Pa." She waves her arms. For a moment he's afraid she'll try to walk through the fire. "Oh, Pa," she shouts. "Come quick."

We're in fire season now in north Texas. It's mid-August, and we haven't had rain since the end of June. The prairie grass turns to tinder; the longhorn cattle chew the leaves from mesquite trees, the only thing still green in the pasture. Grass fires break out. All it takes is a spark – a burning cigarette tossed from a passing car, a loose muffler dragging over the pavement, a rancher's mowing blade striking a rock in a pasture – and something catches the brittle grass, and it starts to blaze.

From my neighborhood on the northwest edge of the city, I sometimes see the black smoke rising up along the horizon. Sometimes the fire's intense heat induces a smoke tornado, a vortex that sucks up smoke and flame. I've seen photographs in the newspaper of these white tornadoes, glowing orange close to the ground, these spirals of smoke churning through the air, their cloudy funnels obscuring whatever lies beyond them. Suddenly it's impossible to see what's on the other side. What a wonder it is. What a horror.

On winter days, when I was a child, my father would drive along our township's roads – perhaps we were on our way to the Berryville Store, or to visit my grandmother, or to the Lukin School for the annual Christmas pageant – and out across the snowy fields we would see the chimney smoke rising from homes, some of them hidden down long lanes. That smoke would be the sign that the people who lived in those houses were safe and sound. If ever we didn't see smoke, we knew there was trouble: illness or poverty or worse.

In the summer of 1978 Brad and I shared an apartment. This was the summer when the woman who would later become his wife, and then his ex-wife, called things off with him. Every time he saw her out with another date, it hurt him, but I'm not sure someone would have known that unless that someone happened to be living with him and saw how, late at night, when the two of us were alone in the apartment, he sometimes went quiet – a rarity for Brad, since he has always been one of the most effervescent people I've known – and stared off into space, having traveled to some secret, inner place.

I had a similar place inside me. Deb was an hour and a half away, acting with a repertory theater company in Vincennes, Indiana, and though I drove down and saw her on the weekends, I secretly worried that at the end of summer, caught up in the glitz of theater life, she would refuse to come back to me.

Although Brad and I occasionally spoke in earnest about our pains and fears, we also understood the importance of keeping each other from falling too far into our respective caverns of gloom, those dark chambers of the heart where we could get lost and never return. We brought each other back with humor and hijinks, some of them adolescent enough to be embarrassing to recall now: ringing telephones answered with boyhood one-liners ("Joe's Bar and Grill"); midnight commando raids on another friend's house, letting ourselves in through an unlocked back door, creeping upstairs, sneaking through the dark house until we pounced on our friend in his bed and shouted like maniacs.

And why? For the pure joy of it, for the idiotic laughter that came bubbling up from the gut, filled the chest and throat, that laugh-until-you-cry glee we remembered from when we were boys.

I was an only child. I had lived with my parents and then Deb. I had never lived in a college dormitory, never gone away to camp, never been a member of a fraternity. That summer with Brad was as close as I had ever been to having a brother. And what an excellent brother he was: companion, confidant, comedian. His booming laugh could fill a room, could catch me by surprise no matter how many times I had heard it. My god, how could anyone love life so much? He had a knack of making people feel better about themselves, a skill that served him well in his career as a school psychologist working with troubled children. I can't imagine anyone who could help but feel they were damn lucky to know him.

The summer of 1978 ended happily for both of us. Deb came home. Brad and his girlfriend got back together. The next summer they married. A few years later they had a child, a daughter, and our circle of friends, four couples, went on seeing each other at Christmas, at shared vacations arranged in various cities across the county. Then, in the early 1990s, Brad's wife filed for divorce, and as sad as that was for those of us who loved them and their daughter, even this coming apart seemed amicable. Brad and his wife arranged joint custody, agreeing that they would do everything they could to make the situation as easy as possible for their daughter.

The years went on. Brad became engaged to a woman who is as full of zest as he is. On the night of the explosion she was staying with her mother, who was ill. Since it was a weekend, Brad's daughter normally would have been home with him, but she was with her mother and stepfather, sailing on Lake Superior.

In the most recent photo I have of Brad – a photo he sent with last year's Christmas card – he and his daughter are sitting on the floor in front of their fireplace, their black lab between them. Brad's daughter is twelve, and even though she's wearing braces on her teeth, she's smiling with abandon, unashamed, a smile so much like Brad's own. The two of them have a shiny garland of red and green Christmas tinsel wrapped around their necks, a glittery strand linking them. It would be clear to anyone, even a stranger, that this father and daughter adore each other. The old sparkle is in Brad's eyes, the glint that says anything is possible.

Eight days after the explosion I found a report in the on-line version of the *Chicago Tribune*, a report from the Illinois State Police Crime Lab that jarred me. Deb wandered into the room.

"There's news," I said. "Someone deliberately cut the gas line to Brad's kitchen stove."

"Murder?" she said. "Who would want to murder him?"

"Not murder," I said. "They found blood throughout the house. The lacerations on Brad's arms happened before the explosion. They're on the insides of his arms, from his wrists to his elbows. The police are using the term 'progressive suicide.'"

How surprised John is when he gets to the house and sees Ursula and Matilda Fite. Ursula has on an apron. She's a tall woman with a long neck. Tendons stand out along its length when she strains to lift a pan of dishwater. Matilda is shorter but just as lean. She's sitting at the kitchen table paring potatoes, her small hands working with speed and grace; the peelings come off in long spirals and fall into the pan on her lap.

"Mama sent us," she says to John. "She said you needed help."

"All the way from Indiana?" he says. He's stunned for a moment to know that there are people in the world who would go to such lengths – uproot themselves from home – all on his account.

"Yes," says Ursula. "All that way."

Louisa is at the fireplace raking out the ashes the way John has taught her. An ember pops and lies glowing on the hearth. John sees Louisa reach down with her fingers. He starts to shout, "No, don't. It's hot." But before he can speak, Ursula has reached out and snared Louisa's hand. She speaks to her in a kind, motherly tone. "Oh, honey. You don't want to touch that coal. It's hot as sin. You don't want to burn yourself, honey. You come on over here and help me dry these dishes."

John lets all the breath that's gathered in him come out with a sigh. A few years later he'll remember this moment, and he'll think this was the instant when so much began to change. Ursula took Louisa's hand and saved her from fire, and so many things became possible, because for the first time since Lizzie's death there were women in the house. John knew – had known most of his grown life – it was women, good and decent and earnest, who had always taught men what it meant to have a family and a home. Without women, men were lost. They were the cold water slapped on the face come morning, the ticking of a clock when no one was in the room to hear it, the gray ash of a fire long burned cold.

On this day, when the Fite sisters have come, they make soap. They pour lye water into a kettle in the yard and build a fire beneath it. They let the lye come to a boil, and then they test it for strength. They set a fresh egg on the surface, and it floats; they dip a downy feather into the boiling lye, and the feather's down and shaft dissolve. Soon there will be cakes of soap – brown, soft soap that makes John's skin tingle when he uses it, that leaves its lye smell on his clothes when Matilda or Ursula washes them. It is soap that cleans in a snap, that eats away dirt, that makes you feel as bright as a new penny.

The trees are full of bud-swell. Soon the leaves will unfold like babies' wrinkled hands reaching up from cradles, and by the time the trees are full and the tobacco starts are growing in the fields, Henry will marry his sweetheart, Mary Ann, and buy a twenty-acre plot of his own. One by one, as the years go on, John's boys will set out on their own. Jackson will marry Matilda Fite. Robert will marry

Ursula. Cousins and sweethearts, as was common in that place and time.

Shortly after the last wedding, when it's once again John and Louisa alone, he goes to the Brian Cemetery, and there he sees Eliza Phillips, a widow for three years now, come to put chrysanthemums on her husband's grave. It's autumn, just past midday, and the sun is high and warm. The wind moves through the golden leaves on the hickories. A squirrel chatters in the high branches, disturbed by the presence of these two humans.

Eliza is kneeling by Ed's grave. John offers his hand to help her to her feet. She takes it without hesitation, and they stand a moment, her palm across his. He's sixty-four years old now; she's twenty-eight.

"It's Indian summer," he says to her.

"Yes," she says, "but winter's coming."

He hears the misery in her voice. He thinks back to that day by her kitchen fire when his breath came out in a sob and she was so tender with him. He covers her hand, holds it between his two, and she doesn't move to withdraw it.

How lucky they are, he thinks, to be here on this sunny day, two people who, despite all they've lost, still believe in love.

"Winter comes," he says. "It goes. It doesn't kill us."

"Sometimes I get so lonely," she says. "Don't you?"

And he tells her, yes. "Yes," he says, "I do."

They marry in April, a season of daffodils growing up from the warming earth. Surely people talk about the thirty-six years' difference between them. Surely there are family members who shake their heads. But who are these naysayers – who are any of us – to say what sparks and blazes in another person's heart, in the secret chambers where longing flames?

Brad, dear friend, I don't know what happened in your life to make you want to leave it, but I'll wager it had something to do with love, though few will believe me.

I've heard that the police have a letter that you wrote to your daughter, a letter that they found lying on a neighbor's lawn after the explosion. I imagine that letter's graceful flight – blown high above the flames that night, a patch of white fluttering like a moth, tumbling down and down past all the chaos to lie, finally, still and safe, on the green grass.

Sort through the rubble, sift the ashes, turn the bones, and that's what we'll find. It's what we always find – the words that survive, the yearning, the knowledge that sometimes, in a dry season, you can want your life so badly, all you can do is set it on fire and let it go.

7
Bastardy

Let's say it was raining. One of those early April rains, cold and bit-
ing, that often fall over Lukin Prairie even now, all these years later,
when the farmers plant in the fence rows, corn coming right to the
edge of the gravel roads, the fields breaking loose and sprawling instead of staying penned in behind barbed wire, as would have been
the case on this day in 1899 – April 5 – when the constable, E. J. Bass,
came riding down the lane on his sorrel mare. "Hie up there, Dolly,"
he said to the horse, anxious to be done with his duty and back in his
house warming himself by the fire. If the temperature were to drop a
degree or two, the rain might easily turn to sleet. Rivulets ran from
his slouch hat. He bent low over the mare's neck as they passed beneath the rain-sodden branches of the hickory tree. He smelled the
sassafras trees, tannin running in the roots, and the wood smoke
curling from the chimney at the Martin place, atop the gentle rise of
the hill, where the maples were starting to leaf out and the cows were
lowing, bags full of milk this close to evening.

I imagine the scene this way because this is the landscape of my
childhood, and the story I intend to tell involves my great-great-
grandfather (although he was dead by the time this all happened)
and his second wife, Eliza, and their son, who is no direct ancestor of
mine, my line already having been set in motion by my great-great-
grandfather and his first wife. Still, when I discovered the facts of this
case in the probate records in the Lawrence County Circuit Court
office, I couldn't help but feel thrilled, but also uneasy, as is usually
the case when we are voyeurs to someone else's trouble.

Eliza heard the mare's nickering, and it put her in mind of her
husband, John Martin, who had died a year ago February, and the
way he used to call to his workhorses, "Comb, comb, comb." The
memory – his voice as clear and as real to her as it had ever been –
caught her by surprise, as if he had suddenly stepped up behind her

to see who was coming down the lane, and she pressed her hand to her throat. If she had to be glad for anything, it was the fact that Johnnie wouldn't have to be here to face whatever was going to happen now. He had died just before his eighty-eighth birthday, "a good citizen and neighbor," according to the item she had saved from the *Sumner Press*, and though it grieved her to be standing there in the house alone, her son John D. – the one they had always called Delbert – out at the barn ready to start the milking, she felt grateful that Johnnie wouldn't have to suffer the heartache that was hers now. She would be the one to bear the sorrow and whatever shame or pity people might cast her way. Better her than Johnnie, she thought, because she had hardened herself to being talked about. Mercy, how people had talked when she married John Martin and escaped her widowhood. "Let them," she had said to her mother and father. "I've got four young'uns to raise up, and Johnnie's a good soul." He had taken to her four as if they were his, and then together they had brought four of their own into the world: Cora and Anora and Lula and John Delbert, for whom she knew the constable, E. J. Bass, had come.

She stepped out into the rain, not even bothering to tie a bonnet around her head. E. J. Bass rode the sorrel into the yard, and Eliza's guineas squawked and scattered.

"Is it now?" she said.

E. J. Bass coughed and leaned to the side to spit onto the muddy yard. "Clara said I'd find him here. If you want to know the truth, it's her I feel sorry for. Married not even three years now, and to have to know this about her man."

"It's that woman? That Mary Woods?"

"I didn't figure it was no secret."

Eliza had grown up listening to her mother, Elizabeth, tell the story of the winter of 1836. One day in January it had rained and snowed a little in the morning. Then, around noon, heavy black clouds came in from the west. Elizabeth had gone to the well and was toting her bucket back to the house when the wind came up and she sloshed water onto her dress and apron. The temperature dropped so quickly, by the time she got to the house, her clothes were frozen stiff. Her father, out in the feedlot, later said the pond froze over in a matter of minutes, and he had to chip the ice away from the cows' hooves. The mud of the pasture field had frozen so suddenly, the cattle had been held fast.

That was how Eliza must have felt once she knew for certain why E. J. Bass had come, as if she were frozen cold with ice, unable to move, unable to do a single thing to stop what was going to happen to her son.

"He's out to the barn," she said.

"About milking time, I guess," said E. J. Bass. "Don't worry, Eliza. I'll let him finish."

In the barn Delbert had his cheek laid against the Guernsey's flank and only heard E. J. Bass's boots scraping through the straw.

"I reckon it's you," Delbert said. He tugged on the Guernsey's teats and listened to the milk, smelling now of wild onions, streaming into the bucket. "I figured it wouldn't be long before you paid a visit."

"I've got a warrant here." E. J. Bass unbuttoned his coat and took the warrant from inside his shirt, where he had put it to keep it dry. "You know it's my job."

"I don't hold it against you."

"Don't go holding it against that girl either. She was good enough for you once, I reckon."

"What's that warrant say?"

E. J. Bass coughed again and spat. "Whereas Mary Woods of Lukin in the said county, an unmarried woman, has this day made complaint upon oath before George W. Peters, a Justice of the Peace in and for said county, that she is pregnant with a child which is likely to be born a bastard and that John D. Martin is the father of said child, you are therefore hereby commanded to arrest John D. Martin and bring him forthwith before the said Justice to answer to said complaint and to be further dealt with according to law."

Delbert listened to E. J. Bass fold the warrant. "Does Clara know?"

"She does."

"And my ma?"

"Everyone's known it was coming since Mary Woods made the charge back in March."

The Guernsey shifted her weight, and Delbert had to steady her with his hand. "I got to finish this milking."

"Go on." E. J. Bass sat down on a stack of straw, glad to be out of the rain. "But don't say anything. Don't tell me a damn thing that's on your mind. I don't want to be your conscience."

Here's something I've never admitted to anyone. No one knows the truth except me and Benny Toon, whom I swore to secrecy. Benny was a neighbor, a few years younger, who admired me so much I have no doubt that to this day he probably hasn't breathed a word about what really happened that night in the Red Hills State Park. It's been years since I've spoken to him – I live far from that part of southern Illinois now – but in my mind I believe he persisted in defending me until the story eventually faded from his memory.

It edged closer to my own consciousness – the story of a snowy December night in 1974 – twenty-five years later, when I was poking through the probate records in the circuit court office and I found the case of Mary Woods versus John D. Martin on the charge of "Bastardy." I didn't know it at the time, but I imagine now that part of the discomfort I felt as I handled the affidavits, the writs of subpoena, the court transcripts, came not only from the fact that I was peeking into someone's painful past but also from what was once my own deceit, my own encounter with the law. Now I wonder whether a written record exists of my own appearance in the circuit court, when I was nineteen and so thankful for second chances that I was willing to lie in order to preserve the new life my family had found.

By 1974 my father and I had learned how to be kinder to each other. Our home, for the first time in years, was a safe place to be. No longer did we shout ugly words, shove at each other, raise fists, or, in the case of my father, use hooks as weapons. We had lived through that danger, and we knew how lucky we were to be on the other side of it, calmer now, more able to love.

Although I wanted to do nothing to risk the peace my father and I had found, there were times when I would get restless. Our church, the Church of Christ, was so fundamental it offered no young-people programs such as the Methodist Youth Fellowship, and even if it had, the young men and women who attended such programs were not the sort of people with whom I found it easy to socialize. They were, for the most part, farm kids from Lukin, the kids I would have grown up with had my parents not moved from our farm, first to Chicago and then back downstate to Sumner when I was ready to start high school. They had no interest in the sorts of things that interested me: books, sports, music. By this time I was in my second year at a junior college in a town twelve miles from my own, and there I had met the sorts of people with whom I felt an alliance, but they had all grown up together, and it would be awhile before I would feel comfortable trying to fit myself into their group. Instead, when I wasn't attending classes, I spent my time in my own town, where I disassociated myself from friends I had had during my trouble-filled years. I was feeling my way through a new period of my life, trying to figure out exactly who I would be in the years to come.

Often in the evenings I went out driving. I drove uptown past Tubby's Barber Shop and Buzz Eddy's Pool Hall and Piper's Sundries, a half-block of buildings off the main street, Christy, in the shadow of the tall bins of the grain elevator. Most nights there were cars backed into parking places along this street, and their owners – boys whose lives would end up much more troubled than mine – would be sitting on the hoods, the embers from their cigarettes glowing in the darkness. Sometimes I would drive out to the highway and follow it the mile east to Red Hills and meander along the winding roads lined with pine trees. In the spring and summer there would be fishermen on the lake, the lanterns aboard their johnboats casting glimmery swaths across the water. If I parked at Prospect Point and stared out across the lake, I could watch the headlights of other cars moving along the far road, turning into ridges and coves where couples often came for privacy. I watched the headlights go out, and I felt a sharp sadness because I was alone, having lost in the past two years two girls, each of whom I swore to be the single, great love of my life.

It might be easy to believe that what went on in those cars hidden away in the darkness was lurid and carnal, something akin to animals rutting, and sometimes, of course, it was, but it was more true, at least in my own case, that such assignations were about feeling closer to someone than I had ever felt. Often it was enough, more intimate than any amount of petting and groping, to hold hands or to snuggle close. Just the memory of the soft sweep of a girl's hair as she laid her head on my shoulder was later enough to fill me with gratitude. All my life I had been desperate for the gentle touch. I had known the hard steel of my father's hooks, the sting of his belt. Even my mother, the kindest person I had ever known, was never particularly demonstrative with her affection. I knew she loved me; that much was clear from her soft tone of voice, her patience, her encouragement. I rarely recall, however, getting a hug from her or a kiss, particularly as I grew older. I do remember the first time I held hands with a girl and how I luxuriated in the warm, soft feel of flesh pressed tenderly to my own.

So on these nights when I sat alone in my car, usually singing along with Jim Croce songs on the tape player, ballads about love gone wrong and the blues-filled, cry-your-heart-out aftermath, I ached for the girls I had lost – girls with whom I had felt safe and loved. Without them, and without any prospect of someone to take their place, my biggest fear returned – that I would be alone the rest of my life, like the old bachelors I saw uptown on Saturday nights, walking slowly past storefronts, lingering at the barber shop, no one at home waiting for them to return.

It was in the fall that I first became aware of Connie Moore. Even now it's hard to explain what went on between us. She would have been fifteen at the time, and I doubt that I would have ever noticed her – at least not in a romantic way – if she hadn't paid attention to me first. One Saturday afternoon – Indian summer, late in October – when I was playing a pickup basketball game on the outdoor courts at the high school, she asked me if she could wear my hat. It was a tweed pancake hat with a snap brim, like the hat John Lennon often wore, and at the time, with my hair long, it made me look more exotic than guys normally looked in our small town, with their feed caps and the occasional Stetson perched atop their heads. When Connie put on my hat, it was as if she were claiming me, and I let her, even though I knew almost immediately that there could never be anything serious between us.

I knew it most painfully on our first date, when we doubled with Benny Toon and his girlfriend. We went to the Avalon Theater in Lawrenceville to see *The Great Gatsby*. All the times I've read that book over the years, I've never been able stop myself from remembering that night in the Avalon, not because Benny and his girlfriend and Connie were out of place, but because I was the one who was wrong to be there, giving Connie the idea, as Daisy briefly did Gatsby, that there might be bright days ahead of us. I suppose in a way Connie and I were alike, each of us wanting to believe in love, seeking it from the wrong people, but if anyone has anything to be ashamed of, I'm the guilty party. I sensed long before Connie did that we could never have anything more than a dalliance, but I persisted in believing otherwise, trying to convince myself, so eager I was for love.

In addition to the difference in our ages, we had no common interests. The only thing we really shared was the proximity of space. I remember her flirtations as being sweetly innocent, but I don't remember them in any detail, which I suppose testifies to what a brief and insubstantial fancy we had with each other. She was sweet to me at a time when I needed sweetness. So when she told me, as she soon did, that she loved me, I said the same to her even though I knew it was a lie.

By early December she had figured out as much, and as any reasonable girl would, she threw me over – gave me the mitten, as my father always said when a girl told me we were through – and took up with another boy, this time one closer to her own age and more suited for her. At the time I was stunned by how hurt I felt, but in retrospect my reaction doesn't surprise me at all. The day my father lost his hands, and I went to live with my aunt while my mother stayed with him in the hospital, I learned that people could leave me. From then on I was desperate for permanence. I was eager to please. Whatever came into my life that gave me even the least amount of pleasure, I wanted to last. So I followed my nature, even though it was foolish, and I tried again to convince Connie that I loved her, and to her credit – she is, you see, the heroine of my story – she rebuffed me, which made me sad and angry, angry with myself for being so needy.

One Sunday night I told my father I was going out for a drive. Snow was slanting down through the streetlights. "You better stay home," he said. "It's not a fit night."

"It's just a little snow," I said, and I said this without snapping at him as I would have in the days when we had fought.

He was sitting at the dining-room table reading his Bible, a posture I was more accustomed to seeing my mother occupy. He banged his hooks together the way he often did when he needed to turn one of them to the proper angle for picking up a pen or a drinking glass. So often in the past that banging had been the first signal of his anger. But tonight he only plucked up the corner of a tissue-thin Bible page, took it in his hook, and turned it over. "Be careful," he said, and I told him I would.

I picked up Benny Toon at his house, and we drove uptown. The Christmas lights strung across Christy Street – the tinsel bells and the giant electric candles – swayed and rocked in the wind. The storefronts were dark, except for the light of a television playing in the window at Hutch's T.V. and Appliance. A car was backed to the curb there, the motor running. I recognized the Ford Galaxie as belonging to one of Connie's friends, and as I slowed down, trying to sort out the faces I could see in the glow of the streetlights, I made out Connie and her new boyfriend sitting in the backseat. I suppose it was then that the sadness of my life came to me. I should have been thankful for the grace my family had found. I should have been home with my mother, who had always loved me, and my father, who in the end had found a way to do the same. But now I had ignored his warning about the wicked night and was out in the cold, the snow coming harder, mooning over a girl I'd never loved in the first place. I sped up, and my tires slipped a bit on the snow before I got control and headed on out to the highway.

Somewhere in Red Hills, I realized that the car behind me was the car with Connie and her new boyfriend inside. Their headlights in my rearview mirror, coming closer and closer, seemed to be mocking me. We had just passed Prospect Point and started to climb the long hill along the lake to the north entrance when I did a stupid thing. Like all stupid things it seemed like a good idea at the time. I put on my brakes, and the car behind me rammed into mine. We had been driving slowly because of the snow, so the impact wasn't hard enough to hurt anyone. The cars, though, were damaged. My taillight was smashed out; the other car's front fender was crumpled. We all stood in the snow and studied the damage.

"You stopped," the girl who had been driving the other car said, a fact she made plain again when the state trooper came to investigate.

"I didn't," I told him. By this time Benny and I had driven to the park ranger's house to ask him to call the state patrol. I had made up my story and told Benny to stick by me. "I was going up the hill," I told the trooper, "when I started to slide a little in the snow. So I tapped my brakes just a bit, and she was following so close she hit me."

Connie stepped forward, her face red from the cold. She narrowed her eyes at me, and in a clear, loud voice she said to the trooper, "He's a liar. He stopped."

The trooper gave me a ticket for illegal stopping on a roadway; he cited the other driver for following too close for conditions.

When I got home, my father was still at the dining-room table.

"I had a wreck," I told him.

"A wreck?" His voice rose in anger, and he banged his hooks together. "I told you to stay home, but you wouldn't listen."

"Roy," my mother said, her voice pleading.

"Listen," I told him, ready to keep on spinning the lie I had manufactured, ready to say whatever it might take to keep us from reverting to our old anger. "It wasn't my fault," I said, and as I did, an image flashed in my mind, a picture of Connie standing in the cold, snow dusting her hair, just a girl, but not afraid, ready to come forward and tell the state trooper – tell the whole world – exactly what I was.

Maybe Mary Woods was lonely and so afraid that she would be an old maid all her life that she couldn't help but notice Delbert Martin, who was twelve years younger. Maybe she believed that if she loved him hard enough he would leave his wife and be hers forever. All I have before me to resurrect her story are her signature on the complaint she eventually filed and the facts of the case as recorded by the court. The facts are merely the facts; the only glimpse I have at the real story of Mary Woods comes from her signature, her age at the time, and my own story, which took place seventy-five years later.

Mary Woods was thirty-three that day in March 1899, when she made her charge against John D. Martin. I know this from the 1870 Lawrence County census, which lists her as four years old, the second child of John and Margaret Woods of Lukin Township. I have in my possession a copy of an 1875 map of the township drawn from surveys and county records. The map shows the farms, each labeled with the owner's name and the amount of acreage. On the map the J. Martin farm, my great-great-grandfather's, fronts the main road that leads into Sumner, the road that will one day be paved and become known as the Sumner-Lancaster blacktop. From Sumner it's eight miles to Lawrenceville, the county seat, where John D. Martin will be tried for the crime of bastardy.

On March 14, 1899, Justice of the Peace George W. Peters records in a flowing script "the complaint of Mary Woods." She is, as the document states, "an unmarried woman . . . who says that she is now pregnant with a child and that the said child is likely to be born a bastard and that John D. Martin of Lukin in said county is the father of the said child." Her signature is written in a cramped, shaky hand, as if it has taken every ounce of grit she has to form the letters: "Miss Mary Woods." The first stroke of the first "M" begins too far above the ruled line. There are wide gaps between the three words, and I imagine her bearing down, the nib of the pen scratching over the paper as she concentrates on what she's doing. She feels the baby shift and settle; she places a hand over the swell of her stomach. By the time she finishes her last name, the letters bleed onto one another, squashed together, the final "s" barely distinguishable, as if she can't wait to leave the presence of George W. Peters and to let whatever she's set in motion with her signing have its end.

She lives in the home of Mr. and Mrs. Charles Greenwood, where later, as sworn before the court by Noah M. Tohill, state attorney, on the sixth day of April, she will take to her bed, too ill in the eighth month of her pregnancy to make the journey to Lawrenceville. Tohill will show to the court that there is just cause against the defendant, who did "on or about August A.D. 1898 have sexual intercourse with the relatrix Mary Woods and that as a result of said intercourse the said Mary Woods is now pregnant with child." The people summoned to testify in her behalf will number nine, including Dr. George W. Reed.

Nowhere in any of the court records is there mention of her parents, John and Margaret Woods. Perhaps neither was living at the time, though they would only have been sixty-one and fifty-nine, or possibly they no longer lived in the area, though I can't imagine them moving on elsewhere and leaving their unmarried daughter behind. Could it be that they were ashamed of her to the point that they had turned her out and left her to the kindness of the Greenwoods? Had her indiscretion with Delbert Martin, and the fact that she dared make it known to the world, cost her mother and father and home?

I can see her now stepping out into the March chill, a shawl drawn close around her, Mr. Charles Greenwood holding her at the elbow because her steps are unsteady. He feels her lean into him, and for a moment he fears she might faint. But she manages, with Mr. and Mrs. Greenwood's help, to climb onto the buckboard, where she sits looking at the green blades of the daffodils – the Easter flowers – just starting to poke through the wet ground.

"Well, it's done," she says, and she says it with such sadness – such regret, Mrs. Greenwood thinks.

"You've done right," Mrs. Greenwood says. "Whatever mistake you made in the past, today you did the good thing. You poor girl. You poor soul. You could barely sign your name."

My father, when he had heard my version of the car accident, defended me. "Who did they think they were?" he said. "Following so close on a night like this. What were they doing out there anyway?"

"I don't know," I said.

He didn't know anything about Connie Moore or the shame I carried with me. He only knew my lie, and perhaps because he was as eager as I to maintain the peace between us, he was willing to believe it.

"You won't pay that ticket," he said. "You won't admit to something you didn't do."

My mother sighed. "What choice does he have?"

"I'm going to the courthouse tomorrow." My father closed his Bible and looked at me. "You'll go, too. We'll have a little chat with Tom Fielder."

"The judge?" I said, amazed by how far my father was willing to go to support me. My heart filled with love and guilt because I had so easily seduced him with my lie.

I wonder now whether Delbert Martin had a similar gift for persuasion. Did he know exactly what to say to Mary Woods to entice her? Perhaps, after Sunday services at the Gilead Church, he chatted with her awhile, made pleasant conversation the way he would with any neighbor. "It's a new dress you're wearing, isn't it, Mary?" he might have said, just to let her know he was making note of her.

Maybe he even danced a reel or two with her Saturday nights at the Froggeye Schoolhouse; maybe his wife, Clara, encouraged him. "There's poor Mary Woods," she might have said. "As usual, no one to dance with her." I imagine him chatting with Mary as they danced. "It's a fine night, Mary, and you're looking well. No one dances a reel like you do, I swear it's so, Mary Woods." Did he hold to her waist a few seconds longer than necessary after the fiddle music stopped? Did he catch her gaze and hold it with his own so she would recall the moment later when she was in her bed? And if she found small gifts left for her on the cistern stone, where he knew she went first thing in the mornings to draw a bucket of water, how could we blame her for beginning to fancy him, particularly if he was the only man who had ever paid her a speck of mind?

And what was in his head about Mary Woods? What was it that made him have to have her despite the fact that he had only been married to Clara a scant two years? All I have at this point is mere speculation, one theory as valid as another. He loved Mary Woods, had always loved her, but hadn't been able to get past the difference in their ages and had married Clara and let his love for Mary smolder those two years. Or else he was just the sort – a scoundrel – who was out for a good time, no matter whose heart he ended up breaking. Maybe, though, there was something terribly wrong between him and Clara, some soreness of heart that drove him to Mary. Or maybe she seduced him. The truth is sealed away in the passage of time, and all I can know for certain is that somehow and for some reason, that summer of 1898, the two of them found each other and began the story that would end with Delbert Martin brought to trial.

The afternoon my father and I sat in the chambers of Judge Tom Fielder, drizzle was melting the snow cover from the night before. The rain glazed the bare limbs of the trees on the courthouse lawn. Only a few years earlier, we had waited with a crowd of hundreds on that lawn for the molester and killer of an eight-year-old girl to be escorted into the courthouse. "They ought to cut off his balls and feed 'em to him," my father had said to another man. These were the days when the two of us were nearly eaten up with hostility for each other, and we had momentarily found a common ground against this criminal who was so obviously more evil than we.

But in the presence of Judge Fielder my father was patient. He asked me to tell my story, which I did in a meek voice. When I was finished, he took his time defending me, explaining to the judge that I had done nothing wrong and shouldn't be held to blame for what had happened the night before in Red Hills State Park.

"He's had his trouble in the past," my father said. He was sitting on the edge of a leather wing chair opposite the judge's mahogany desk, his work cap held by its bill between the prongs of one hook. "We won't deny that. But he's a different sort now. We both are. If he says he didn't stop on that road, then that's good enough for me."

Judge Fielder was a young man – thirty-five, forty – and I remember him as being attentive but impassive. He pressed his hands together and put the tips of his forefingers to his lips and turned his swivel chair so he could look out the rain-flecked window. "In every case I hear," he finally said, "there are conflicting accounts of what happened. It's my job to listen, to weigh the facts, and then determine the truth. What you want me to do now is dismiss a ticket on the basis of your faith in your son, and while I find that faith admirable, I can't base a decision on it. There is a due process of law, and I have to have the opportunity to hear from the other side as well."

"A hearing?" my father said.

Judge Fielder nodded. "If that's what you decide."

I could see the muscle in my father's jaw tighten, a familiar sign to me of his rising anger. I felt miserable about being the cause of that anger. If I had only stayed home like he had advised instead of going out for a drive – if I hadn't lied – we wouldn't be here, on the verge of an irretrievable choice.

"It *is* what we decide." My father put his cap on and tugged the bill to snug it to his head. His voice was fierce – restrained, but barely. "I told you," he said. "My son's a good boy."

In 1899 there would have been no father to stand by Delbert Martin. That duty would have fallen to his mother, who was indeed summoned to appear before the court. This was all happening at a time when Progressivism was sweeping the country. People believed that they should have more influence in the government and that the government should be more active in securing the public welfare. Women were seeking the vote. Ten years before, Jane Addams had established Hull House, a relief center in Chicago. All through the

1890s women formed literary circles, joined the Anti-Saloon League, attended Chautauquas, where they heard lectures about Pragmatism, which called for a validation of truth by consequences. "The ultimate test for us of what a truth means," William James said, "is the conduct it dictates or inspires."

I can't imagine, despite women's growing collective voice, Eliza Martin being anxious to speak in court, to move toward truth. I imagine that day, instead, as one of the most painful of her already difficult life. Even though I don't carry her blood in my veins, I come from her place – Lukin Township – and I've known generations of women, my mother most of all, who bowed their spirits to the will of men, working alongside them on the farms, bearing their children, having little time for literary circles, Chautauquas, progressive thinking.

Mary Woods was perhaps a different sort of woman – unmarried, willing to risk so much for the attention of a man, bold enough, once she was pregnant, to bring suit against him, to leave a record for someone like me, all these years later, to find.

Whatever Eliza Martin said when she spoke in her son's behalf, it wasn't enough to keep him from being convicted. Nor were the words of Delbert's sisters, Cora and Lula and Anora, who were also summoned. From April 6, when Delbert first appeared in court, until June 8, when he was convicted, the judge granted five continuances while waiting, I assume, for Mary Woods's child – the evidence – to be born. And when that child finally came into the world, the court levied a fine of 550 dollars against John D. Martin, a fine he couldn't pay, nor could any of his family, evidently, since the court sentenced him to six months in the county jail.

My own fate wasn't as dire. In the end my appearance in court was severely lacking in drama. By that time I had lied to the state trooper, my parents, Judge Fielder, my insurance adjustor, the insurance agent for the other driver. I had asked Benny Toon to lie for me, which he was prepared to do that day in court. But he never got the chance. What happened was something probably only I can recall. The other driver and her witnesses, Connie Moore included, failed to appear. Judge Fielder, obviously only too glad to clear a case from his docket, called me to the bench and explained to me that, because the other party hadn't appeared, he was willing to dismiss both tickets that the state trooper had issued.

"Does that sound all right to you?" Judge Fielder asked me, and I didn't know how to answer. I had no idea what was right anymore. In a sense I was being rewarded because I had lied, had refused to pay the ticket outright, and had forced the hearing. In a sense the other driver and Connie Moore were saving me with their silence, a silence Mary Woods hadn't been able to convince herself to keep. For a moment I was as mute as Delbert Martin must have been when called to answer the charges against him. Judge Fielder was waiting. He leaned toward me. "Well?" he said.

The siren at the fire station was sounding, as it always did to mark the beginning of the noon hour. It was time for lunch, and clearly the judge and the court reporter and the state trooper who had come to testify were anxious to get to it. To them my case, now done, was merely an uninteresting ripple in a long ocean of cases. But to me, then, and even now as I look back on it, my future with my father – our happiness as a family – hung in the balance. I remembered all the times my father and I had fought: the night I had stolen his car, the day he had caught me shoplifting. I had disappointed him and my mother time and time again, and just when we had reached a peace – just when my father and I had learned to live kinder lives – I had gone out on a snowy night and put all that at risk for the sake of a girl I didn't love and who knew I didn't love her. I heard something squeak behind me, and I knew it was the harness of my father's hooks. I turned to look at him and saw him leaning forward, one hook reaching out in front of him. I thought of the times he had shaken that hook in front of my face, even pressed its point into my throat one night and pinned me to the wall.

"All right," I said to Judge Fielder. And then we were done.

Now I wonder what happened to Delbert Martin when he finally got out of jail on December 8, 1899. Did his marriage to Clara survive? Did his mother and his sisters somehow get beyond their shame and forgive him? Did Mary Woods ever find happiness? And what of the child – hers and Delbert's? Did it ever know the story that I do now?

I choose to know it the way I know my own, as a tale of fault and redemption. Once Judge Fielder had dismissed my ticket, my father gave me money for lunch. "You treat Benny to a hamburger," he said. He was in a jolly mood, happy, it was clear, that we had, as he said, "won the day." He touched me lightly on the shoulder with his hook. "Go on, now," he said. "You don't want to hang around with us old folks."

My father would live eight years more. He would see me marry, graduate from college, begin working. Those eight years would be everything the other nineteen should have been, years of love and respect between a father and his son. He saw me turn into an upright citizen; I saw him become a more gentle man. I never told him the truth about what happened that night in the Red Hills State Park, that I had indeed stopped on the roadway, causing the accident. He would never know how close we had come to returning to our own disaster.

When Benny and I stepped out of the courthouse, the sun was shining. It was a weak, winter sun, but a sun nonetheless.

"You got away with it," he said, and, as had happened when Judge Fielder asked me if I thought it was all right if he dismissed my ticket, I didn't know how to respond. The court record would always state the fact that the ticket had been dismissed, and I would be, at least on those pages, an innocent man. What I felt inside was that no one gets away with anything, that every action has a consequence, but I didn't want to give words to what I was feeling, afraid that I would destroy the other thing blossoming inside me, a tremendous thanksgiving, convinced, as I was, that I stood ready to step fully into the rest of my life. If I were to talk to Benny about the incident now – if he even remembered it – I'd tell him that if I had the chance to tell the lie again, I would.

On that day all I said to him was, "I'm hungry. Man, I'm starved."

We walked down the courthouse steps, under a gray sky tinged with swirls of violet and blue, a sky that could go dark any minute or break into full sun until we would have to squint to see our way.

There may have been similar light the day Eliza Martin died at the home of her daughter Mrs. Anora Meyers, in Tuscola, Illinois, some one hundred miles north of Lukin Prairie. It was a Wednesday, February 13, 1918. Delbert Martin would have been fifty-one, no longer a young man who had made mistakes and paid for them. The child he fathered with Mary Woods, if indeed it had lived all this time, would

have been nineteen, the age I was when I appeared before Judge
Fielder, close to the age Delbert was when his life intersected with
that of Mary Woods. I'd like to believe that they all found grace
somewhere back in the ages beyond my reach.

The last fact I have about any of them is a copy of Eliza Martin's
obituary, which states that "the remains were brought to Sumner
Friday noon by her son, John D. Martin, and wife and daughter."
Though I'm tempted to say that the wife referred to is Clara, and the
daughter theirs, I have no facts on which to base this conclusion. I
could, if I chose, go back into the census records and search for an
entry for a John D. Martin and wife Clara, but I prefer to leave the
truth murky, to allow just enough room for the possibility that the
woman traveling with Delbert that day in 1918 was Mary Woods, and
the daughter their own, the child whose birth nineteen years earlier a
court had awaited, thinking, when it was finally born, "Here is the
child, come at last. Look on it now, and say what's true."

8
The Voices of Children

Stella knows it's happening again; a child has taken life inside her. She's missed two monthlies, and she wakes these mornings sick to her stomach. She hides the sickness from Will, sneaking off to the privy before he's awake, afraid for him to know.

Then one morning he's there on the path when she comes out of the privy, wiping at her mouth. The sky is just beginning to lighten in the east, back through the black branches of the bare trees. In the field behind the privy, the dry cornstalks scrape their leaves together. Hoarfrost crunches beneath Will's feet as he steps toward her. He lays his hand flat against her stomach.

"You're in the way," he says, and at first she thinks he means for her to step aside so he can pass. Then he presses against her stomach, and she realizes that he knows.

"I reckon I am," she says.

"So we're to try again, are we?"

She places her hand on top of his, and together they hold warmth to where the child lies. "Looks like that's what God means for us to do," Stella says.

Will tips his head forward until it touches the top of hers. "Praise God," he tells her.

"Yes," she whispers. "Praise God."

This child is my father, and he comes to Will and Stella after they've buried two babies, each in their second summer. No death record exists for the first child, Lola, but my aunt has told me that she died of summer complaint, a digestive ailment common in warm weather, when foods stored in the milk house sometimes turned and grew bacteria. The same illness claimed the second child, Owen, in 1912. His death record shows that he died on August 24 at six A.M., after two days of acute indigestion and twelve hours of convulsions. His age was one year and two months.

In the photograph I have of Owen, he's wearing a white gown with a lace hem. Someone has propped him up on a chair covered with a fur rug. The gown's hem trails down to the floor. Over halfway up its folds, Owen's little feet press against the cloth. He stares at the camera with a pained expression, his eyes squinting, furrowing the skin in the middle of his forehead, pinching it into the worry line that all the Martins will wear, even I, nearly a hundred years later. Where did it begin? With Henry? Or further back, with John? Or was it Will, who in photographs always looks so glum? Will, with his deformed right hand? Will, who watched his first wife, Ella, mother to his boy Glen and his daughter Mae, waste away with the consumption?

Glen, at the time of Owen's death, is a young man of twenty; Mae is seventeen. They are each amazed by how quickly their lives are moving ahead. Eleven years have passed since their mother's death, and here they are watching their half sisters grow. Ferne is nine; Edna is six. They have all mourned Lola's and Owen's passings, but in different ways: Ferne and Edna with a child's bewilderment and hollow ache (*Our baby's gone?*); Glen and Mae with the more adult sense of how vulnerable they all are. The babies' deaths remind them of the night when they were the ages of Ferne and Edna and they crept to the edge of the loft and watched their mother's hand go slack and the splinter of the chicken's wishbone fall to the floor.

Now Glen is about to marry Fern Mabus. His grandfather, Henry, has helped him buy acreage to the north, the farm that will one day be Mack Jent's. Mae is sweet on Harry Brubeck. Glen and Mae, motherless, have always clung to each other, have always felt themselves somewhat apart from their father and Stella and the family they are raising now.

When I study the penny-postcard photograph that Glen and Mae had made of themselves shortly after they both married their sweethearts, I imagine how distant they must have felt from my father's birth, perhaps even resentful that it hadn't been their mother, Ella, bringing this brother to them. In the photograph, despite their gay attire, no joy lights their faces. Glen is in a pin-striped suit; a silver stickpin adorns his tie. Mae wears a hat with a sash around it and a spray of flowers at the left side, where the brim turns up. She has a beaded necklace around her throat. A dainty purse dangles from a chain that she grasps with her hand. They are young, in good health, and gussied up for the photographer, but their postures and their somber faces suggest that there will always be a sadness in their lives. They have lost their mother, and what will ever be able to make them forget that? Glen, tall and rawboned, sits in a chair, his back straight. Mae stands beside him, her torso tilted slightly toward him as if to say, this is who I've always counted on; this is my brother.

In another photograph, the one taken when their half sister, my aunt Ferne, was no more than three, she and Mae and Glen are in a line. Again Glen sits in a chair, his arms crossed in defiance; Mae stands next to him, barely holding Ferne's hand, as someone has surely told her to do, looking as if she would rather be anywhere but where she is.

I have no memory of Mae, only her name, *Mae Brubeck.* My father always said it as one name, and perhaps that's why it left an impression on me. Surely he must not have felt close to her; otherwise he would have called her Mae.

Glen I remember because he thought that television was sinful, and when he came to visit us, I had to keep our set turned off, missing my favorite programs. He was a severe man with loose-fitting dentures that clacked around in his mouth. Though my father appeared to enjoy those visits, when Glen was gone, he spoke of him in unflattering terms, speaking of how prissy he was, how odd, how judgmental. It seems likely to me now that no matter how congenial these half brothers tried to be to each other, there couldn't help but be tensions between them – Will Martin's first and last sons, each from a different mother.

All day, after Will has surprised Stella coming out of the privy, he thinks of the child growing inside her. He feels Ella's presence, and he remembers how young she was when she gave him Glen, just seventeen. That night, when Will lies beside Stella in bed, he says, "Ella always gave Mae and Glen a spring tonic. Sulphur and molasses. She said it thinned their blood and cleaned out their systems and got them ready for summer."

Stella smoothes her hand over the quilt, the wedding-ring pattern she and her mother sewed. "Are you saying the other two was my fault? Lola and Owen?"

"I'm only saying what Ella did."

"I know what Ella did."

"All right, then. Good night."

After my father died, and my mother had gone to live in a nursing home, I sold most of their belongings at auction. Among the items were my grandmother's quilts, butter molds, kerosene lamps, her rocking chair, her treadle sewing machine – all the things that had passed from my grandparents to my parents. I sold them because Deb and I lived in a small apartment in a part of the country where we knew we wouldn't stay. Deb was in graduate school. Who knew where the years would take us or how many moves we would make before we finally called someplace home? I had gone away from Lukin Township, and on the day of the auction, I carried away only what I could fit into my car: my grandmother's Depression glass, the rocking chair I used as a child, two boxes of family photographs and mementos, a small table someone in the Martin family built. How I wish I had back everything I let go, particularly those quilts, so I could feel the stitches Stella made as she sewed together the blocks, those scraps taken from old dresses and shirts. If I could only look upon those patterns and colors. I remember sleeping under them as a child; their weight on a cold night was a comfort. *Comforters*, my mother called them. The blocks were smooth with wear and pleasantly cool to the touch, like a pair of familiar blue jeans, faded and soft. It was nice to lie on top of a quilt in the summer and so cozy beneath one when the snow was blowing outside and the winter wind was rattling the storm windows. Why didn't I keep just one, perhaps the wedding-ring quilt, the pattern of interlocking rings symbolizing eternal unity? At every turn I'm the betrayer of my family. I write this as my penance.

All winter the weight of the child fills Stella with joy and dread. She remembers Lola and Owen and how there was nothing she could do to save them. She listens to Ferne and Edna's chatter and thinks there's nothing in the world that lifts her spirits as much as the voices of children – so musical, so full of life. Did she revisit all this when I was born? Though she would have been nearly blind with cataracts then, I'm sure she knew me through my cry, my sweet baby scent, the feel of me in her arms, which would have been the weight of all her babies, those she had lost and those she had saved.

I've never lived around babies, but I can imagine the substance of their presence, a presence that any parent must know as fragile, something they must eternally guard. But I'm on shaky ground here. I'm only speculating. I can't remember ever holding a baby in my arms.

It's not that I haven't had chances – younger cousins, children of friends – but I've always shied away, even though I've wanted a baby's weight, wanted the feel of tiny fingers tapping on my face, wanted the attentive gaze of liquid eyes or the comforting rhythm of their breathing as they sleep. I've wanted to hold life at its beginning, to know better, perhaps, how precious we all are, to know that we have all been, no matter the mistakes we've made, at one time inno-cent and without blame. But something has always held me back. Maybe it's just the fact that I've feared that if I hold a baby in the presence of others, they will immediately find me unworthy. The baby in my arms will call attention to what I'm not – a father – and I will be found wanting.

Sometimes in daydreams I imagine the child Deb and I might have had if our circumstances had been different. As a boy I always longed for a sister, so in my daydreams our child is always a girl. A baby girl who lies in her crib and reaches up her hands to me, who clings to my fingers, her arms stretched over her head, her belly pooched out, her dimpled legs bowing as she learns to walk. And then one day she sits on my lap, and I read to her the way my mother read to me, and my daughter lays her head against my chest, and I lean over and kiss her on her head, and I know this part of my life, closed to me now – the joy of ushering my child through the world.

But I have other daydreams as well. I see my daughter sobbing because another child has said something mean to her. I see her lag-ging at the edge of a children's activity, clinging to my hand because she's timid about joining in. Or, worse yet, I see her throwing temper tantrums, or as a teenager, screaming at me with defiance, leaving home, finally, and never coming back. How my heart would break, and even so, I would gladly take the chance.

"It's all risky," I've told Deb. "Every bit of it."

When we first began talking about one day having children, she admitted that the idea of pregnancy terrified her. I couldn't blame her for feeling that fear. It was genuine and rational, given the effects pregnancy has on a woman's body. Deb, from time to time, mentioned the possibility of adoption, an alternative that I at first dismissed.

"You're like all men," Deb told me. "You're egocentric. You want to duplicate yourself. You want an heir."

All right. Guilty. I admit it.

But as the years passed, and we remained childless, being a progenitor became less of an issue. I realized that at the heart of my inclination toward fatherhood lay the desire to open myself more fully as a human being, to become less egocentric by diminishing my own concerns for the sake of those of my child.

"All right," I told Deb. "Let's adopt."

"Why?" she wanted to know. "What's made you change your mind?"

I tried to explain my thinking as clearly as I could. "And besides," I told her, "I'm afraid we'll end up with a lonely life." I was thinking of my mother, alone after my father died.

"Having children doesn't guarantee they'll be there when we're old," Deb said. "We weren't there for your mother, and now we aren't there for mine."

She was right. All that was true. But would our mothers have preferred not to have had us at all?

Did Stella wish my father hadn't come? Did Will?

He says again to her, "Good night."

She turns her back to him and holds her hand to her stomach. Soon he has crept close, has wrapped his arm around her.

"I guess I'm just scared," he says.

"Children do that," she tells him. "They make you afraid on account they're so wonderful. How can you hold them? How can you keep them alive? Have you ever listened to their voices? Really listened? It's like singing, like angels singing. They make you feel all small and big at the same time."

This must be what every mother has felt, every father as well. It's what Deb and I will never know.

"We've done what we can," I told her. "My mother, yours."

"Yes," she said. "But we haven't done enough."

I imagine Stella and Will huddled together, not speaking, knowing there's nothing left to say. There will be months of hope and fear, and this is what will tell them they're alive. In the quiet night, as they slip into that netherworld of almost-sleep, they can hear a faint chiming as delicate as glass. Perhaps, as the ancients believed, it's the music of the spheres, the harmony of the planets vibrating as they spin through the heavens, or maybe it's the voices of their children: the long-ago prattle of Glen and Mae, the babble of Lola and Owen, the chirping of Ferne and Edna, the sounds my father will make. Perhaps, in Stella's womb, a humming starts to stir.

9
A Quickening

By January Stella is swollen with the child; my father quickens inside her, shifting and turning in the watery dark. I imagine his fingers beginning to form at the ends of his tiny hands, the ones he'll one day lose. But for now they're safe; for now my father dozes through winter, through the short days of cold and snow, through the long nights when by five o'clock Stella has lit the kerosene lamp and Will has finished his milking by lantern light.

"Supper?" he asks when he comes up from the barn, his face red with the cold, a few snowflakes melting on the rim of his milk pail.

"Soon," says Stella. Then she tells Edna and Ferne to stop picking at each other. "Or I'll send you off to bed without a thing to eat," she says. "Won't you fuss and bawl then?"

Perhaps my father hears the hum of these voices. Perhaps he listens to their drone – so close they seem and yet so far away. He is as drowsy as a bee in a hive, drunk on honey, and oh, so warm, so content to stay exactly where he is.

The crape myrtle at the corner of my house blooms in late July and keeps its color – almost pink, almost purple – long into September. Delicate stems, tinged this same color, connect the blossoms to the berries from which they've unfolded. But the blossoms, though freed from the berries' tight orbs, are crinkled and papery. If I roll one between my fingers, it wads up like a piece of damp tissue.

The yellow jackets and wasps come to feed on the honeydew glaze that aphids have secreted on the crape myrtle's leaves. My study is at this corner of the house, and as I write, I hear the wasps humming. Such a busy noise they make, as if they're frantic to be heard as they go about the business of being wasps.

Their proper name is "social wasps," because they live in colonies, their nests holding anywhere from two hundred to five thousand of them. Social wasps build their nests from wood pulp. They use their mandibles to scrape fibers from weathered wooden fences, barns, telephone poles. These insects then chew the wood, using their saliva to moisten the fiber, then adding the paste to the nest and spreading it about, sculpting it with their mandibles and legs.

What patience it must take, the wasps' whiskery legs skittering over the wood paste. Not exactly trowels they're working with here. Some ancient instinct must fill them with faith. They keep moving because nature has made them thus. Little by little they build nests the size of a man's fist or, if they must, a bushel basket.

But we, perhaps less perfectly made, fall prey to all sorts of fissures in mind and soul. We sink into these cracks – some of us are agoraphobics, afraid to leave our homes; others are manic, consumed, finally, by our attraction to constant and irresistible stimuli, like moths drawn to flame or June bugs batting their heads over and over against porch-light globes. Sometimes we never make it back to the world. And all the while the social wasps work on, scraping minute bits of fiber from the structures we have so confidently erected – our fences, our very homes, perhaps – because to them these things are only wood, and that is exactly what they need, and surely they won't take enough for us to ever know.

Each morning, after he's done the milking and carried in firewood for Stella's stove, Will crosses the road and walks up the lane to his father and mother's house. He's glad to see the wisps of smoke coming from the stone chimney. Mary Ann is usually sitting by the fire, reading from her Bible. This same Bible will lie for years at the bottom of Stella's wardrobe, along with boxes of family photographs, but only a few pages will survive. I have them now, pages upon which various people have recorded the births, marriages, and deaths of Ridgleys and Martins, beginning as far back as George Ridgley, born in 1799, and stretching on past Lola's and Owen's deaths to Stella's own in 1965, recorded in my mother's elegant hand.

Mary Ann, who will die in 1919, bends at the waist, holding her face close to the Bible. "He's out to the woods," she says to Will, not bothering to raise her head. "I told him he was a fool."

"The woods?" Will says. "On a day like this?"

"He took the broadax. That's all I know."

Will follows his father's tracks through the snow that has fallen overnight, a wet snow that clings to the cedar and pine trees and dusts the rail fences around the farm lots. Will tracks his father to the rear of the garden plot. A hobnail must be working its way loose from Henry's boot, the left one, because Will can make out the shape of its round head where it pressed into the snow. The air is fragrant with wood smoke. A jay is screeching from the top of a sweet gum at the edge of the wood lot. Will steps up the stile and crosses the fence into the corn brake, where the stubble pokes up through the snow and the dry husks, pale and curled, litter the furrows. He remembers how he and Glen shucked the corn last fall and hauled it to the crib in his father's barnlot. "I reckon I can still bring in my own crop," Henry had said. But it was clear to Will that his father's eyes had started to fail. Now he worries about him in the woods with his broadax. Stubborn, the old man is. He fought a war, survived a prison camp, built his house, his barn, his granary and henhouse, his smokehouse and milk house – built everything with his own hands, even split the rails and fenced his pigpens and calf lots and garden patch and barnlot and dooryard.

"Everything was kept up," my aunt Ferne told me once. "That farm was always a showplace."

It will be six years, at Mary Ann's death, before Henry will deed the eighty acres to Will, but already Will has been imagining what he might do with the land – twice what he owns across the road. His brother, Charlie, who owns the forty acres to the south, has built a frame house – no rough-hewn logs for him – with a picket fence around the dooryard, a fancy latched gate opening to a plank walk that leads to the front door. Will has always envied his brother, envied his striking good looks, the slim-waisted wife who dotes on him, his whitewashed frame house, bright and shiny on the hill to Will's south. Fortune has marked Charlie Martin. He won't spend his life beaten to death by farm work. By 1920, at the age of forty-nine, he'll be a clerk in a dry-goods store, leaving the farm to his son's blood and sweat.

It's Will that Henry will turn to when his eyes are so bad he can no longer see to hitch a team of horses or to use a corn hook. Now Will tries to fathom what he could be up to out in the woods with his broadax.

When Will steps into the wood lot and sees him down the slope where the creek runs, he stops, as still as a deer who has sensed danger. He is afraid to go farther because he has happened upon something so private it stuns him.

Henry is standing by a cedar tree. He has cradled a bough with his hand and is just now lowering his face to the needles. Will feels an ache in his throat, an ache similar to the one that filled him the night he knew that his first wife, Ella, would die and again when God took each of the babies, Lola and then Owen. He knows that Henry is sniffing the needles, feeling their scratch on his face, because he can't see well enough to know that this is a cedar tree. And, too, there's something loving about the way he holds the bough, the way he nuzzles it, as if he's saying hello to an old friend, as if this intimacy is of no shame to him after all his years of walking this land. Will knows that his father loves the cedar tree as he does the wood lot and the creek and the pasture beyond it, where each summer the timothy grass grows. He loves every acre, every rise and dale as the land rolls out to his fence lines. He loves it enough to come out in the cold and snow, near-blind as he is, because he is somehow wedded to all of it. Will knows this because he has learned the features of each of his children, has traced them with his fingertips: the clefts in their chins, their pug noses, the oversized ears he swore they'd never grow into. He has taken his children inside him the way Henry has this farm.

"Dad," Will says, but the word comes out in a whisper. "Daddy," he says again, this time louder, and he's surprised by how young his voice sounds, how timid.

Henry lets the cedar bough go and jerks his head toward Will. "Charlie," he says, and Will feels his heart sink.

"No, Daddy," he says. "It's Will."

"Oh, Will. Good," says Henry. "Come help me cut down this tree."

"What do you want to cut down that tree for, Daddy? Christmas is come and gone."

At Christmas, for as long as Will can remember, he's gone into the woods with Henry and cut a cedar tree to tote to the house. Even after he and Charlie had married and set out on their own, Henry had insisted on having a Christmas tree. "I believe it lifts your mother's spirits," he told Will back in December, "just to see it putting on a show." They draped the tree with strings of popcorn, cranberries, red haws. They tied little red apples, saved since fall in the milk house, to the branches. They hung walnuts and hickory nuts and gourds and the ruby red ears of Indian corn. Mary Ann tied ribbons into loops and hung them on the tree. By the light of the kerosene lamps, the ribbons and apples and cranberries and Indian corn brightened like jewels. When Will brought Ferne and Edna for a visit, Henry helped each of them cut an apple or a nut from the tree. "That's to hold you over," he told them, "until Santa Claus comes." And when it was finally Christmas, there were play pretties for them: spinning tops that Henry had fashioned by inserting a peg through the holes of an empty thread spool and whittling it to a point, building blocks he had made by splitting corncobs, whistles he had carved out of hickory bark. How he loved to watch the girls' eyes open wide with excitement and their mouths come open in disbelief. "Go on, honey," he told each of them. "Take it. It's yours."

There is danger in what I'm doing, calling up the dead. I touch them with a hesitant hand, as if they lie sleeping beneath quilts. Their voices come to me, muffled and faint, as they are this day in the snow-filled woods. Here they are, my grandfather and great-grandfather, men I never knew, and yet I miss them terribly. Their resurrection, a feat I've engineered, makes me yearn for them all the more. That's the danger of opening doors into the years before I joined the living; I discover the traces of all I've missed, all I'll never have. I discover family. My imagination both pleases and torments me. I pass down long hallways that veer at sharp angles. Those before me throw shadows on the walls. I arrive too late, stepping into the stir of air they've left behind.

I imagine the broadax in Will's hands: the haft lathed from hickory; the wide blade cast from iron and honed to a sharp edge. Over sixty years later I'll stand in these woods chopping down a cedar tree for our Christmas because my father at the time will be recovering from his first heart attack. When he finally ventures out into the cold, he'll wear a papery blue surgical mask over his mouth and nose to keep from breathing the sharp air that would make his blood vessels constrict.

Through the generations of Martins, there has been a closing down, a lessening of offspring. John Martin, with his two wives, fathered twelve children. My father and mother never meant for me to appear, but I did, and now that I am childless and will remain so, unless fate has something different in mind, I will fulfill the destiny that my father and mother intended, the end of our part of the Martin line.

"I'm going to make a cradle for your baby," Henry tells Will. "That's why I want this cedar tree."

Will, the broadax lifted and arcing down now in midswing, turns to look at his father, and the haft twists in his hands. The blade strikes the cedar trunk with its flat face, and Will feels the vibration in his arms. The tingle is so sharp that he drops the ax in the snow.

"My baby?" he says.

Henry stoops over and feels about in the snow for the ax. The last time he worked with cedar was when he built Owen's casket.

"That's right," he says. "That grandbaby Stella's carrying." He finds the ax haft and lifts it from the snow. He holds it out to Will. "The world lets us start over," he says. "I had to go through a war and walk away from a prison camp to learn that. And now I'm telling it to you."

But he doesn't have to tell it. Will is remembering how when Ella died he thought he'd never be able to put one foot in front of the other, but he did, and then there was Stella and love again and babies, and now, not even six months since Owen died, another baby is making ready to come to them. The snow will melt into the creek come spring, and the freshets will flood the bottom land and coat it with rich silt. Come summer the corn will stand above a man's head, tassels reaching up to the sky. But now Will has a cedar tree to cut, and Henry has a cradle to build. There are these things, no matter the sadness people carry with them, to get done.

There was a time in my life when I nearly lost myself to depression. It was 1981, and I worked for a federally funded program called Educational Talent Search. The program targeted individuals who were either economically, culturally, or physically disadvantaged, but who also demonstrated an interest in and a capability for postsecondary education. It was my job to visit high schools and social-service agencies in search of people who with a bit of a boost (I could offer career counseling, admissions assistance, financial-aid counseling) could put themselves into a college, a vocational school, even beauty college, and by doing so improve their chances for productive, happy lives. I went into county probation offices, halfway houses, children's homes, YMCAS, Catholic Charities, Goodwill, St. Vincent DePaul, the Salvation Army. Every day I met people who were in trouble: teenagers whose parents had thrown them out of the house, kids who had suffered sexual molestation, people who had lost their jobs, people who were physically disabled. I came to know thieves and junkies, abusers and their victims – all manner of people whose lives, for one reason or another, had exploded. I caught the fragments and carried them inside me, never able to forget the women with bruised faces and black eyes from a husband's or a boyfriend's beating; the twelve-year-old girl whose brother had raped her; the gaunt, ethereal boys, their frail arms scarred with needle tracks. Some of them were con artists, feigning enthusiasm for my services just to see what they might be able to swindle: money, rides, a place to sleep. Others were grasping at straws, any boat in a storm. I could count on one hand, after three years, the number who had actually gone to school and set their sights on a better way of living.

For the most part I spent my days listening to one sad story after another, and the only balm I could offer, outside my own empathy, was, in the short run, ineffectual: career-interest inventories, financial-aid forms, college-admission applications. All of my efforts pointed toward something far in the future to people who were worried about the here and now, people who were frantic for food or shelter or drugs, people trying to avoid violence, prison, their own compulsions, and I knew there was little I could do to help them.

Many of them could barely keep still while they talked to me. They jounced their legs, popped their knuckles, bit their fingernails. They paced the floor, swiped shaggy bangs back from their eyes. Their lives were crazy, they told me again and again. I wouldn't believe it, they said. Man, they'd landed in a mess.

I think of them now when I see the wasps, frantic at the crape myrtle, hovering and jitterbugging from leaf to leaf, landing to sip from the honeydew, and then lifting off, held aloft by their gossamer wings.

This evening I notice a nest beneath the eave, wasps clinging to the comb. I remember how I retreated into my home when the sadness of those lost people became too much for me. I silenced myself to my wife, I ignored family and friends, I became ill with chronic bronchitis – a convenient excuse for staying home from work. I was eager for some long sleep, for a sweet remove from the world.

Was this what my friend Brad felt the night he opened the veins in his arms, cut the gas pipe to his kitchen stove, and lay down on his bed? He must have yearned for a slipping away. I search and search for why this would be so. The only clue that surfaces is the information that he was slow to recover from an appendectomy that spring and was depressed over the inflammation that left him in pain and kept him from the physical activities he loved the most: skiing, tennis, golf. His doctor prescribed painkillers, and now a friend speculates that too strong a dose or a combination of the drug and alcohol may have led Brad to a psychotic episode. It happens sometimes with painkillers – the Elpenor syndrome, named for the companion of Odysseus. Elpenor woke from a drunken sleep and leapt to his death from a great height.

Was that it? Was it some malfunction of brain chemistry that loosened Brad from his sanity? It's one story, and, of course, there are others that we try out. Did he simply lose himself to the weight of all the kids he treated? All those broken lives. All those damaged children. Did they become too much for him? Or was it some old wound he had carried with him for years, some hurt or slight or loss that led him to despair?

Earlier that summer he and his fiancée had gone to Hawaii with the intention of getting married, but they didn't. They came home, still engaged, no wedding date set as far as I know.

This is the summer when Deb and I will reach our silver wedding anniversary. Toward the end of July we sent Brad and his fiancée an invitation to the celebration we're planning for August. All along we've been aware of how fortunate we've been over the years to keep passing by all the doors that would have led us out of our marriage. Others, such as Brad, haven't had that same luck, and though I don't want to claim any undue significance in his story, I can't help but wonder whether the timing of our invitation coincided with some sadness he was feeling because his own marriage hadn't panned out the way he had always hoped.

His night of horror took place a few days after what would have been his and his ex-wife's twenty-first anniversary. Although he had

gotten on with things, fallen in love again and started looking ahead
to the future, did he also carry some sense of failure?

So many circumstances. So many possible narratives. I don't claim
that any of them can explain what Brad did. They are simply the
splinters of bone that I rub, hoping some marrow might still be stuck
to them, anything that might help me understand.

All I know for certain is that one summer night he decided he
would no longer carry sorrow in him like a coil of chain, links
threaded down his throat to lie, finally, in the pit of his stomach. He
would simply go to sleep; he would leave behind his daughter, young
and healthy, nearly thirteen, ready to blossom into a young woman,
vibrant, her face aglow with her father's smile.

But everything went wrong. The gas leaked out into the house and
exploded, and there was Brad, who had never meant to survive this
night, alive for the firefighters to find and save.

A week goes by, and then two, and Brad is still alive. It becomes
convenient for me to believe, as each day ends and no news of his
death comes, that he will survive. I believe this because I don't want
to believe its opposite. And at the same time I feel a bit of anger flare
in me. How could he do this? How could he, who had spent the last
twenty-two years helping kids in trouble, bring so much pain to so
many people who love him? He dedicated himself to helping children in need. Now what about the need he has created for his daughter? I tell myself that I have no right to his inner life – no right to put
his story on the page, but I can't keep myself from imagining those
last hours when he gave in to whatever despair tormented him.

I see him, now, pressing blade to skin, wincing at that first sting
but keeping at it, slicing along the underside of his left forearm
(right-handed, he surely would have done the left arm first), letting
out the blood – the quickest way, he thinks, to get this job done. But
it isn't quick enough, not even after he cuts the vein in his other arm
(a ragged job, having to work with the left hand), so he moves
through the house. Is he amazed that his feet still step one in front of
the other? Is he angry that he's still walking on this earth? Does he
weep as he goes to the front door? Investigators will find it later,
blown across the street, its inside surface smeared with blood.

I imagine him at that door, and it's here where time slows down,
where everything hangs in the balance. He leans his arms against the

door, lightheaded now, perhaps considering. I want him to open that door and go out into the night, lift up his voice in a wail until someone comes running. I want him to hold out his bloody arms and say, "Look. Look at what I'm doing." I want him to laugh that familiar, gut-rattling laugh and say, "Can you believe it? Geez, what a dope." I want him to be amazed, in love suddenly with the night air, and the feel of grass beneath his feet, and the weak hearts of people stupid with grief.

If I can make him open that front door, make him call out for help, I can save him.

But he doesn't, and I can't. He turns away, moves to the kitchen, blood leaking out onto the floor. He turns on two burners on the stove, lets the gas rush to their jets. He bows his head over the stove – investigators will find blood there, too--breathes in, but there's not enough gas to do the trick.

He's impatient now. All this is taking much too long. So he pulls the stove back from the wall and goes out to the garage to fetch his hacksaw. There, he lets his dog – the black lab – out of her kennel, turns her loose in the fenced yard. Neighbors will find her the next morning, dazed, her fur singed into curls as fine as baby's hair.

Brad returns to the kitchen. He kneels behind the stove. Does he remember the prayers he said as a child? All the times he knelt and opened his mouth so the priest could lay the communion wafer on his tongue? He uses the hacksaw to cut the gas line. Such a methodical, determined sawing, going at it with purpose, steel blade cutting through copper.

When he finishes, he leaves the hacksaw on the floor. He climbs the stairs to his bedroom. Why not just lie down on the kitchen floor and breathe in the gas? He's weary now, worn out. Is it the comfort of his bed that he seeks? He lies there and waits for the gas to fill the house. Then he'll drift away into nothingness – the black swirl he finds preferable to whatever torment has become too much for him to bear.

He holds his secrets inside him, and when he finally wakes, covered with fire – the gas ignited by a spark from the air conditioner clicking on or the telephone ringing – he'll lose the chance to say them. In the hospital, burned so badly, he'll be unable to speak. The architecture of his despair will crumble and flame, and those of us who love him will forever try to reconstruct it. If we can build it, we can figure out why we couldn't see it. We're left with hope, finally, which fights against the reality of Brad's condition.

When the human body burns, it loses fluid; the volume of blood circulating at the sites of the burns falls, and in an attempt to compensate, the body draws fluid from its uninjured areas. In the first forty-eight hours after a severe burn, fluid from blood vessels, salt, and proteins passes into the burned area. Blood pressure drops; urine output is low. Then the body reverses itself, and a shift of fluid in the opposite direction results in excess urine, high blood volume, and a low concentration of blood electrolytes. Essential body cells suffer. The liver and kidneys cease to function properly. Circulation begins to fail due to a lack of oxygen in the tissues. If someone dies from burns, he dies from the inside out.

Through the middle of August, while sap runs in our crape myrtle and helps it put on its brilliant blossoms, Brad's internal organs go into shock. The prognosis for his survival is poor, but still the days go on. One evening, over the telephone, his fiancée tells us that today, as she sat with him, his eyelids fluttered when she spoke, that they opened just enough for her to glimpse his blue irises. We hold this news – those specks of blue – as hope. As one friend puts it, "At least we know he's in there." What we don't know, I think, is whether he wants to be.

Then, on August 28, his blood pressure drops drastically, and at 8:20 that evening, he dies. The journey he began twenty-eight days before is finally at an end.

Deb and I travel to Illinois for the funeral, and what surprises me, as it always does, is how vivid the world becomes at the time of loss, how something close to joy can circulate among those who mourn a death. Though we don't speak of it, surely I'm not the only one who notices the stained-glass windows at the Catholic church, backlit with morning sunlight, or the wooden pews, bright with varnish, cool and smooth when we touch them. I have hugged our friends, luxuriated in the solid substance of their bodies. I hold Deb's hand in mine; it's been a little over two weeks since our silver wedding anniversary – twenty-five years – and sometimes we've forgotten how to love each other, and sometimes, like now, we know exactly why we've chosen to keep moving through the world together. We are joined in partnership, true to our original vow to finish the journey, to see each other through whatever we have to face along the way. Love is what lifts us up, heals us when we are in need of healing, and perhaps, for reasons we'll never know, this is what Brad felt that he had lost.

But he has given it to us, as ironic as it seems. His leaving has brought us here, where burning incense emits a pungent smoke as the priest swings the censer on its chains, passes it over Brad's casket to bless the spirit spiraling now, thinning as it rises into the air.

To make the cradle from cedar, Henry cuts the runners with his drawing knife and then curves them while the wood is still green. He carves out the lengths he'll peg together to make the cradle's bottom and sides and ends, no nails on which a baby might scrape an arm or leg. Will reads the measuring stick, marking the cuts, then helping Henry use the wedge and mallet to split out the heart, the old, hard center that's no longer living and is impossible to work.

They build a fire in the barnyard under an iron kettle and wait for the water to boil. When it does, they drop in the lengths of cedar wood and set them to cure. The boiling water will draw out the sap from the wood pieces, and then, after they're out of the kettle and the water has evaporated, they'll be seasoned and ready to use.

"I reckon we'll keep at it up into the night," Henry says. "That ought to cure that cedar good."

They piddle around in the barn, mending harness and coming back to tend the fire. Just before noon Henry says to Will, "Hadn't you ought to let Stella know what you're up to?"

It troubles Will to know that he has been enjoying the morning spent away from home, that Stella and the girls have been far from his mind. He has cut the cedar wood, glad for its clean, sharp scent. He has put his thoughts to measuring out the exact lengths, to watching his father auger the holes and whittle the pegs while the wood is still green and unlikely to split. Henry's fingers have lingered over each peg, gauging by touch what he can no longer see well enough to gauge with his eyes. And Will has marveled at his father's patience--how he caresses the wood – and his obvious delight that he has lived long enough to make this cradle. Now he has had to remind Will of his duty to this family, and Will is ashamed of the thought that comes to him. It surprises him so that he speaks it to his father: "I'm not sure I want this baby."

Henry pokes at the fire with an old broomstick, and the hickory splits settle. "You don't know what you're saying." An ember lifts up into the air and pops. "You're talking a fool."

"I lost two babies," Will says. He can still feel the weight of them in his arms.

"You think you're special that way? You think you're the only man ever lost a young'un?"

"No, Daddy. I know I'm not, but I'm scared. What if we lose this one, too? I think it would ruin me."

"Of course, it'd ruin you." Will thinks of his father shaving the cedar wood, trimming and smoothing the rough boards with his drawing knife, the wood curling back from its blade, each pass taking more and more. "It's what living does to us. Nigh on forty-four years old, and you don't know that by now? Ruins us a little bit at a time."

"I know it." He thinks of Ella gone, of Lola and Owen. "That's what scares me."

"Don't you know the other? The part that saves us?"

"Tell me, Daddy."

"We're all being ruined at the same time. Getting cured up good, and we know it. That's how we take to each other." He pokes at the boiling water with his broomstick, nudges the cedar boards. "Sap's leaking out this cedar now. Smell it?" He sniffs at the cold air. "There's always something sweet in ruin. Ain't no cause to be a-feared. You go home. You tell Stella we're making this cradle."

When I was a small boy, my mother, who was tone-deaf, sang me to sleep each night. She sang "Rock-a-Bye Baby" in a thin, shy voice, and I sensed, even then, that this was something she wouldn't be able to do if there were people watching her. It was a private moment between a mother and her son, a moment she loved enough to forget that she couldn't sing worth a dime. When she looked at me in my bed, did she think me a miracle, a son come to her so late in her life? I'll never really know, but I imagine that she could barely believe the turn her life had taken – an old-maid schoolteacher, married at age forty-one, and now a mother.

I write this on my forty-fifth birthday, the age my mother was when I was born. It's a bright morning in Texas. The wind chimes outside my front door set up a merry tune, and the wasps flit about our crape myrtle tree. The leaves rustle; the ornamental flag my wife has hung from a staff on our house unfurls and pops in the wind. Soon there will be cooler days and bright orange pumpkins and corn shocks and straw bales on people's lawns. Halloween is coming, and our neighborhood, full of young families, will overflow with trick-or-treaters – beautiful children, some of them made more stunning (princes and princesses) and others made grotesque (witches and extraterrestrials).

Yesterday, as I was chatting with our neighbor, his son came out of the garage on roller skates, calling out, "Dad, look at me." I felt the way I always do around my friends' children, aberrant and bereft, knowing that no child will ever say those words to me.

As much as I say that I'm at peace with the fact that Deb and I are childless, there are still moments such as this when I'm painfully aware of the joys we're missing. Just to hear that word, "Dad" – I can only imagine what it does to a father. Or does it, like any word heard again and again, lose its power? It wasn't enough to keep my friend Brad alive. He chose to put that word and the beautiful daughter who said it away from him forever.

For Deb and me our "children" are our students – usually graduate students – who become more than that. The ones who spend time in our home, housesit for us when we're away from town, remember us on birthdays and holidays. We're thankful for the music of their voices when they're all chatting away at one of our parties. Our house comes to life then. It seems brighter, more cozy, more a home.

I think of the wasps' frantic buzzing that I hear as I sit in my study; they must be nesting under the eave or up in the attic. Perhaps their hum isn't frantic at all, rather a content murmur. Perhaps I'm hearing the daughter queens who live through winter, hibernating in attics, basements, tree trunks. I think of babies cradled in treetops, Moses nestled in his ark in the bulrushes, my father afloat in his amniotic sac that winter of 1913. It strikes me that my birth is nearly equidistant from today and the day of my father's birth. Forty-five years have passed since my own; forty-two years elapsed from the day he was born until the day he became a father.

When Will steps into his house, Ferne throws her arms around his legs. "Daddy," she says. "Daddy, Mama's took sick."

Will sees Stella then, curled up on her side in the bed where Ella died of the consumption. Little Edna is beside her, clinging to her back.

"Stella," Will says. His heart is thumping because he's afraid something's gone wrong inside, something with the baby. "Honey," he says, "what's ailing you?"

"Mommy's crying," Edna says. "Uncle Charlie come and Mommy started crying."

Will kneels beside the bed. He remembers the night Ella died, how she was so hungry. She broke the chicken's wishbone with Stella, and her end, the short one, fell to the floor. Will started to go after it, but she grabbed his hand. He found himself reaching out his other hand for Stella because his body already knew what he had yet to admit – that he would cling to Stella, this girl who had nursed his wife and children, the rest of his life.

Her hands are covering her face now. He has to gently pry them away, and it breaks his heart to see her eyes, puffy and red, and her cheeks wet with her crying.

"Stella," he says again. Her shoulders are shaking. He puts his hands to them and feels them heave. "You got to tell me if something's wrong. Something with the baby."

Her face puckers up. Will remembers Lola and Owen and the way they looked when they went into convulsions. "The baby," Stella says. "My baby."

"What about it, honey?"

"Go ask your brother," she says. "Let Charlie tell you what's wrong."

Charlie is in his parlor listening to the player piano he ordered from St. Louis last Christmas. "It's a Welte-Mignon," he told Will the first time he showed it off. "You order up these rolls of music," he said. "You put them on this spool here and then pump these pedals, and the air turns the spool. Just look at those keys jump."

Today the piano is playing "I'll Take You Home Again, Kathleen." Charlie is sitting in his Morris chair, the back reclined, his hands locked behind his head. Clara is sitting on the piano stool; her dainty feet, the toes of her shoes barely visible beneath the hem of her dress, press the pedals that force air into the player. She is so thin, so slim of waist and hips, it's difficult for Will to believe that she gave birth to the boy Omer, who is now fifteen. Years later my aunt Ferne will point to his photograph and say, "That's Omer. He was the black sheep."

Clara wears her hair pinned behind her head, and her long neck is so graceful, her back so straight, as she sits on the stool. Will has spent more than one evening sneaking glances at that long neck, wondering what it would be like to put his hands to it. And what has always confused him is the conflicting desires he feels – to stroke that lovely neck or to close his hands around her throat as if he were wringing the neck of a chicken.

When Ella was sick with the consumption, Clara wouldn't come to see to her, for fear, she said, that she would catch the disease and carry it home to her darling boy. Will has never forgiven her that, nor has he forgiven Charlie his good looks or his fine house or his handsome son or the fancy player piano, the Welte-Mignon, filling the house now with its rollicking, happy tune.

Will grabs the roll and pulls on it until it tears. The house is suddenly quiet except for the torn end flapping once, twice, against the spool and the click of Charlie's Morris chair coming back into place. "What in the hell's got into you?" he says to Will, who is wondering the same thing. What in the hell, indeed.

He holds the scrap of the music roll in his hands, his fingers feeling, as Charlie had invited the first time he showed him the Welte-Mignon, the perforations, the tracks of slots, each space containing a separate note of music, and he feels something kindle inside him, something he can only call belief, for standing here now, beholding the fearful looks on Charlie's and Clara's beautiful faces, he understands that already they dread their old age – God knows what end of sorrows Omer will bring them – that whatever happiness they've managed is as fragile as the paper he now holds, this paper made from wood fibers boiled and pressed, given now to swelling and rotting with any extreme in temperature or humidity. How easily it came apart, so easily that it's clear to Will that everyone, no matter how beautiful or blessed, is afraid.

Knowing this, he feels a great calm settle over him. He thinks of all his family who have lived on this earth; sometimes he goes out to the cemeteries – Brian and Ridgley and Gilead – just to lay his hand on their stones, to trace the letters of their names: John, Elizabeth, Nancy, Ella, Lola, Owen. If he could, he would retrieve them, gather their bones and bring them to Stella, tell her the end of their story has been worked out since the beginning of time. "Turn it any way you like," he'd say, "and this is what we leave behind. All of us. Why should we let our living make us afraid?"

But that isn't true, not exactly. My mother and father come to me in dreams; awake, I find them in the way my body feels when I sit in a chair, walk across a room, bend in my garden to push seeds into the soil. It's as if their bones have come into my skeleton. When I climb my ladder to remove the paper nest the wasps, dying back after winter's frost, have left beneath my eave, I remember the way my father climbed a ladder, bringing each foot to rest on a step before moving up to a higher one. My own legs have learned this motion. I will carry it to my death, and when my bones have gone to ash, the way my parents moved through the world – the musculature of their bodies – will vanish forever.

"What did you say to Stella?" Will asks Charlie. "What did you say to make her cry?"

Charlie bows his head. He presses his hands together as if he's about to pray. "I told her good luck." He raises his head. "Honest, Will. That's all I said."

Will lets the scrap of the piano roll drop to the floor. His strong hand, the left one, before he's even thought what it's doing, moves to Clara's neck. He feels her head tip back at his touch, her spine stiffen. Fingers trembling on his crippled hand, he removes the pins from her hair and lets them slide into his palm. Her hair falls down her back. He has seen the hair of the dead, woven into loops and curls and framed on silk beneath glass. He has seen the sick and the dying, their hair loose about their shoulders. His hand still at her neck, he turns Clara's head so Charlie can see her face, can imagine her in Ella's place the night that she died.

"You said it out of meanness, didn't you?" He lets loose of Clara's neck. His good hand strays to her hair. His fingers comb through its fine softness. "You knew it wasn't what a woman who had lost two babies would want to hear."

Charlie rises from his chair. "Let Clara be."

"I'm not hurting her. Am I, Clara?"

Something happens so quickly then that Will couldn't stop it even if he was of a mind to. Clara reaches up and takes his hand, which is still combing through her hair. Gently she untangles his fingers. "I'm sorry," she says. She brings his hand to her lips and kisses it. "I'm sorry for all you've suffered."

At that moment Will forgives her for turning away from Ella. He forgives Charlie for what he said about the baby. He forgives God for taking Ella from him, for taking Lola and Owen. He forgives himself for telling his father earlier that he wasn't sure he wanted this baby to come.

The hairpins in his right hand tumble to the floor. "Nothing to be sorry for," he says. "We're all doing the best we can."

At our silver wedding anniversary celebration, I paid Deb the penny she had loaned me twenty-five years before when I hadn't had enough money to pay for my lunch. I asked the band to play "Pennies from Heaven," and when they were done, I took the microphone, and I told the forty or so friends who had gathered to help us celebrate the story of the penny and how I hoped that Deb still thought it the best investment she had ever made. I said that it had certainly brought me a lifetime of riches. Then I asked Deb to join me in a dance, and the band played the song we had used as the recessional at our wedding, Jim Croce's "Time in a Bottle":

> *I've looked around enough to know*
> *that you're the one I want to go*
> *through time with.*

I had known it that first night when we talked over coffee at Art's Truck Stop. Deb had known it, too. And though there had been times over this quarter of a century when, given a little less perseverance, a little less love, we might have walked away from each other, here we were, sliding into an embrace as easily as we had when we danced at high-school proms and spring formals. Here we were, as we were then, facing, alone, whatever the future might bring us. And the couples who watched us, or who joined us finally on the dance floor, knew in the privacy of their own hearts the give and take, the will and accommodations necessary to keep love alive.

How fortunate any of us are to survive our own living. Our nesting is often tenuous, as lightweight and frail as the combs the wasps build, meticulously rounding and joining each cell, where a brood will form and eventually emerge, wings taking to the air.

If I close my fingers and squeeze, surely the structure will collapse, turn to dust. But it proves to be surprisingly elastic. Unlike the piano roll that Will tore so easily, the comb folds in the middle but doesn't break. I stretch it back to its original shape. The cells are intact; their papery walls hold.

Will steps outside, into Charlie's dooryard, and he sees the smoke rising from the fire at his father's. To the west of it another trail of smoke spirals up from the fire at his own house. He imagines Henry poking at the cedar wood with his broomstick, standing there nearly blind, seeing in his head how when the pieces are dry he'll fit the pegs to the holes. He'll paint the seasoned wood. This is what he'll do, build this cradle on faith that Stella will bring this baby into the world and keep it alive, this baby who will be his last grandchild. Will feels himself buoyed up by this faith. His steps quicken as he sets off down the road.

The wind is out of the east, and he knows that another snow is coming. The worst of winter will soon be upon them. But then there will be spring, and the summer, and the new baby come to them. He feels confident of that now. He thinks of the faith it took for his ancestors to cross the ocean, settle in Pennsylvania, move on to Kentucky and Ohio and finally here to Illinois. He understands that there are still generations and generations to come, starting with my father, who has quickened to life and waits now for his entry into the world. It saddens Will somewhat to think about the worlds and worlds of people who have preceded him, and those who will come after he is gone. A flake of snow lands on his face, and he feels it melt away. How insubstantial any one of us truly is. But oddly enough this knowledge also heartens him. He'll tell Stella not to worry about what Charlie said, not to fret over a thing. "Whatever happens," he'll say, "let the ones who come after us worry. Let them wonder what they missed on account they never knew us." He'll tell her about the cradle and how he and his father will make it. They'll cure the wood, let it dry, and then peg it together. They'll set it to rocking, this empty cradle, and wait for the child to come.

Here's something I've never told anyone but Deb. On the evening before Brad's funeral, I left our hotel and went for a run. I ran along a country road on the dusty shoulder. Cornfields stretched out to the horizon, the stalks starting to pale and ready for the harvest. I ran against the traffic so I could see the cars coming and so their drivers could see me.

One of the cars was an old American Motors Pacer, nearly identical to the car Brad was driving years ago when we stopped at a restaurant and came back after dinner to find the car gone. Someone had stolen it, and now, twenty years later, it came toward me on this highway, and the driver, who looked enough like Brad to startle me, gave me a friendly wave as he passed, speeding along this road in northern Illinois where no one knew me.

Usually when I run I pay scant attention to the drivers of the cars that I meet. What was it that made me look at this driver, made me see his winning smile, his resemblance to my dear friend, now gone?

I don't have the answer, but the questioning tells me this. We should keep our eyes open; the dead come back to us. Or perhaps they never leave. They're in the tobacco plants growing along a hillside in Kentucky; in the hickory nuts fallen to the ground in an old country graveyard in southern Illinois; in the timothy grass waving and rolling in the wind; in the delicate clavicle of a wishbone; in a *Little Pets* linen primer I've framed along with my father's baby shoes; in Kentucky Wonders, their tendrils lush with beans; in the silence that settles over our house each night when Deb and I lie down to sleep.

The dead can come to you in a squat blue car. Its driver can give you a jaunty wave and then speed on, leaving the wind rushing around you as you turn and watch the car vanish, racing ahead to a destination, somewhere that you aren't meant, for the time, to know.

10
Sight

One morning in 1920 Henry finds himself riding in his son Will's Model A. It's late August, and they're on their way to Hamilton County, where Henry's brother Jackson lives. Through his cataracts, Henry can make out the bright sunlight, dappled by dark patches of trees, gray skeins of wire fence, looming humps of hills. He can smell the dusty scent of the prairie grass starting to die away, can feel the air beginning to cool after the hot summer. He doesn't want to get his hopes up, but inside he's as excited as he was when he was a boy and he left Ohio with his family, wondering what all he would see on his way to Indiana and then on to Illinois. He's scared, too – as scared as he was during the war – though he won't let on. What a wondrous thing, Jackson has told him after his own operation, to be able to see again after all these years.

"Another few miles and we'll be to McLeansboro," Will says. "Daddy, how you riding?"

"Tolerable," says Henry. "Stella, how about you?"

Henry has always fussed over her, admiring the way she stepped in when Ella was sick and Will needed help.

"Don't fret over me, Daddy," Stella says. "Roy's keeping me entertained."

My father is reading from his first primer. Henry has felt the soft nap of its linen pages. Roy likes to lay it in his lap and guide Henry's fingers over the words. "That's 'sun,'" he might say. "Can you feel it, Granddaddy?"

The letters have no raised edges, but Henry never wants to disappoint him. "Yes, I can feel it," he always says.

Roy's reading a story now about a fisherman:

Do you go by the sea?
Yes, I do.

I saw a man.
Was he an old man?
No, he was a big man. He had a net and the net was wet.
How did the net get wet?
In the sea, but the man can dry it in the sun.

"That's no trick," says Stella. "You've known those words a good long while." Roy starts to read the story again. "Be still," Stella says. "Your Granddaddy doesn't want to hear you rattle on."

"Let him read," says Henry. "He makes me see things."

Because he's nearly blind, Henry likes to close his eyes to shut out what shapes and light he can still detect, choosing to see what he can remember. And what he always sees first is that day in 1865 when he came home from the war and there was Mary Ann, picking pole beans in her grandmother's garden. She had filled a bushel basket and was gathering the last of the beans in the pouch she had made by lifting the hem of her apron. She was no longer a girl. She was sixteen, and she worked with a deliberate purpose, snapping off the beans, gathering them, one, two, three, four, before dropping them into her apron.

How right it was, Henry thought, that she should be the first person he saw – she, the one he had told that evening at the box social that he was going to enlist. "I'm going off tonight," he had said. Maybe, he thinks now, he was wishing in some secret part of himself – some cavern he didn't even know – that she would tell his father and put a stop to it all. But she didn't, and before dawn he made good on his word. He sneaked out into the dark and made his way to Lancaster and joined the 130th Illinois Infantry.

He had seen men in the war blinded by minie balls or artillery explosions. How thankful he was that morning in 1865 to stand in the sunlight at the edge of the Ridgley pasture – to be whole and with clear sight so he could see Mary Ann, the one he had thought of time and time again as he marched through the South and into Texas, had kept on his mind the last few days, walking home from Camp Butler, close to two hundred miles to the north.

And then she turned, as if she had sensed his presence, as if she were a wild animal catching his scent. "Henry Martin," she shouted. She let her apron drop, and the beans went tumbling to the ground.

She ran out of the garden – this is what Henry sees most clearly when he closes his eyes: Mary Ann running out of the garden, into the pasture, her arms held wide, reaching out to him all the long way.

Sometimes I dream my parents back into the world of the living. As I sleep, our spirits arise and walk through my house, out into the backyard, where we stand, admiring my garden. My mother stands with her hands on her hips; my father clasps his hooks in front of him just below his breastbone. Everything about them is familiar to me, as if the years since their deaths haven't passed at all. I wake from these dreams with a lingering sadness that stays with me long into my day.

Because my parents were already middle-aged when I was born, they left me too soon. When I was twenty-six, my father's second heart attack killed him; six years later my mother died. I was thirty-two, nobody's son. Whatever decisions I made from that point on, I would make without the advice of a mother or a father, and without their judgment or approval. It was my show. With the deaths of my parents, I stepped fully into my adult life.

And one thing I carried with me was the eighty acres in southern Illinois that Henry Martin had bought in 1884. He had deeded those eighty acres to Will and Stella in 1919, and they had passed them on to my father, Roy, in 1940. It must have been a disappointment to him when he realized that I had no interest in the place. After his first heart attack in 1979, he talked several times about selling it, but he could never bring himself to let it go. And then he was gone. And then my mother. And the farm that had been Martin land for over a hundred years was mine.

I was a poor and absent steward, content to cash-lease the ground and in essence to let it become another man's domain. In all the time I owned the farm, I lived in four different parts of the country, all of them so far from Lukin Township that I never felt that those eighty acres were mine. I didn't walk the fields and the woods. I wasn't there in autumn when the leaves turned yellow and red and orange, or in winter when snow drifted across the barnlot. I couldn't walk into the house and build fires in the fuel-oil stoves or switch on lamps that passersby on the County Line Road might see glowing in the farm-house windows. All was dark there, night after night, season after season. I lived my life away from Lukin Township, thinking it had nothing to do with me now that I had gone out into the world. Each year I paid the farm's property taxes, collected the cash rent, and only a handful of times did I return to actually set foot on the land that I owned. Every time I did, part of me believed that I had a right to be there, and part of me felt ashamed because I had betrayed the land, had betrayed my parents, had betrayed generations of Martins by deciding to turn my back on farming.

It could have never been a natural way of life for me. For one thing, I lacked the know-how. I had never been interested in listening when my father tried to teach me the mechanics of agriculture, the ins and outs of animal husbandry. I always had my nose stuck in a book instead, or my face up close to the television screen. Had I been born years earlier, in the times of John and Henry – neither of whom knew how to read or write – or in the generation of Will, or even my father, when there would have been no television to distract me, surely my life would have taken the path that theirs did. I would have been a farmer, married to the land and its seasons. But once I had the power of the word – once I had imagination – I was able to write a different story for myself. I saw into different lives, and what I saw had nothing to do with farming.

But in 1865, when Henry came back to Lukin, what else was there for him but the land and Mary Ann – the first, its ownership, the only way he could enable himself to have the second?

He took her hands that day in the pasture when she ran to him. "So you know me?" he said with a wink. "I haven't changed enough to make me out a stranger, have I?"

"I prayed that you'd come back." Mary Ann squeezed his hands. "Every night I prayed on the evening star."

Henry thought of how often, in camp, he had watched the western sky for the first, bright star. To know now that Mary Ann had done the same sealed for him what he had been mulling over nearly every step of the two hundred miles from Camp Butler: he would have her; he would make her his wife. He had bought her pound cake that afternoon at the box social, had choked it down. All during the war he remembered the way she had cleaned the crumbs from his chin with her handkerchief. How gentle she had been, so gentle he hadn't been able to stop himself from telling her his secret, that he was going off to war, his father be damned, and she held the secret as her own, closed herself around it as fiercely as she was now squeezing his hands.

"You could have kept me here, you know." He pulled his hands away from hers. "All you had to do was tell my pa what I meant to do."

Mary Ann shook her head. "And betray you?"

"Or maybe save me," Henry said. "Did you ever think of it that way?" He didn't mean to speak so sharply, but his words came out with a bite, carrying an anger he hadn't even known was his. "You didn't know what was coming," he said, and he tried to say this softly. He tried to say he was sorry for snapping at her. "In the war, I mean. I didn't either. I could tell you horrible things."

"I did what I thought you wanted." Mary Ann's voice was shaking. Her bottom lip was trembling, and Henry feared she would cry.

"I know you did," he said. "We was just kids. But now I'm back. I'm back, and I'm as good as gold. Looky here." He opened a leather purse and showed her the silver coins inside. "It's my army pay," he said. "Have you ever seen as much? It's near enough to buy a piece of ground. For us, I mean. That's what I aim to do."

"You keep your old money." Now Mary Ann was the one who spoke sharply. "Just keep it, Henry Martin. You think you can buy me? I'm not for sale."

This is the moment when the journey back into memory gets as unforgiving and as jouncy as the Model A he's riding in now. He opens his eyes, not wanting to see Mary Ann running away from him that day in the pasture, the grasshoppers stirring up around her skirt. He wants to come back to blindness, but he sees her anyway, sees Mary Ann growing smaller and smaller until she's gone and he's alone in the pasture, the sun bright above him, and he knows he has to move, has to hike on over to his folks' place and face his daddy, with whom he has only exchanged a handful of letters in the time he's been gone, letters Henry paid the company clerk to write for him. The return letters were written in a hand Henry recognized as his sister Sarah's. He imagined his father pacing back and forth as he dictated these letters, or standing at a window staring out across a fallow field where snow filled in the dead furrow where nothing ever grew.

"I fear I've tossed my seed on stony ground," his father said in one letter. "You've betrayed me, Henry. You've failed to take root, and now you've washed away. Though I wish you no harm, I wonder how I'll ever again be able to call you 'son.'"

That was the letter that had hurt the most when the company clerk read it to him; it was the letter to which Henry had no answer, and now he had to face his father because, for the time being, he had nowhere else to go.

Roy is reading from his primer again:

We go in.
So do we.
I go up.
So do I.

"Are we almost there?" says Stella.
"Yes," says Will. "We're almost there."

I know there were times when my father was ashamed of me, and rightly so, because for a while, when I was a teenager, I was a shoplifter, an arsonist, a burglar, a drunk. I was, my father told me again and again, on a one-way train to ruin. Perhaps it's a sad comment on me to admit that now I can forgive myself those crimes. I was young. I was stupid. My father's beatings had filled me with a rage that I had to let loose on the world. To this day what pains me, though, is that after my father and I came out the other side of our difficulties – after we learned to love each other with kindness and respect – I disappointed him one more time.

I could blame the trouble on love, but that wouldn't forgive what I did. It was the spring of 1976, and I had just finished my junior year in college – "finished" meaning only that the academic year had come to an end and I had limped along with it, my spring-semester transcript showing the three courses I had withdrawn from, an "F" in educational psychology, and an "A" in modern drama. I had dropped the courses because I had missed so many classes I knew I could do nothing but fail. I had foolishly imagined that I could at least pull a "C" in ed psych. Modern drama I had loved from the beginning, due in part to the professor, a woman as kind and as patient as my mother, a woman who took an interest in me and spent extra time during office hours helping me better organize and express my thoughts. I seriously doubt that I would be writing this now if not for her presence in my life. Her name is Lucy Gabbard, and she is the teacher who made all the difference for me simply because she was willing to take the time.

But even she, that spring of 1976, couldn't keep me from disaster. It was the first year of my marriage, and my father was paying our rent and our tuition. He was investing in me, and though I wanted to do well – wanted to please him – I was also, at the age of nineteen, away from my parents' dominion for the first time. I was married, head over heels in love, and my classes were often low on my list of priorities. I acted as if I were on vacation, and it shames me to think of how Deb worked at a fast-food restaurant while I skipped classes to play pinball in the student union, or to sleep, or to play my guitar, or to do anything but what I was supposed to, which was to go to class and study and get a degree so I could be a high-school English teacher and keep Deb from having to come home with her skin smelling of hamburger grease and my father from feeling he had thrown his money down a deep, deep well.

I was an idiot all the way around, and I can't forgive myself by saying I was young. I turned twenty that year. I was a husband. I should have been a stand-up man, someone people could count on. But I was a wastrel instead, a fool on a path I thought I could navigate. Each day I convinced myself that I would make a turn and get back to right living, not knowing that I had lost my way a good while back. I was like a man deep in the woods on a moonless night, feeling about with his hands, trying to see exactly where he should go.

Over the course of my lifetime, I've had to do things I didn't think I could survive. One of the most difficult took place on a morning in May 1976. A few days before, my mother had called to say my grade report had arrived in the mail. Both she and my father were very disappointed. My father didn't think he could go on paying rent and tuition if this was the way I was going to behave. I felt as if I were fifteen again, and I knew it was right for me to feel that way. I withdrew from the university, and Deb and I moved back home.

On that morning in May we drove down to my parents' farm, where my father was planting soybeans. I walked out to the field where his pickup truck sat, the bed loaded down with sacks of seed. My father was at the far end of the field, riding atop his tractor, his hooks glinting silver in the sun. He braked at the end of the field, raised the planter, and turned the tractor. He set the planter down and started back toward me. As he got closer, I heard the chains on the planter clicking along. I filled two buckets with soybeans, and when my father stopped at the end of the row, I went to him, the buckets heavy, my steps clumsy and halting over the tilled earth.

My father was high above me, his face grizzled with whisker growth and flushed red from the sun, the same sun he had worked under all his life. He was almost sixty-three years old, and he looked weathered and worn. He hammered his hook against the tractor's steering wheel, turning the hook so he could get a better grip on the wheel's spinner knob. It terrified me to think how he would soon light into me about how foolish I had been.

But when he spoke, his voice was soft, almost embarrassed. "Make sure you fill them even," he said. After the heartache and shame, that was all he had to say to me, and that was the moment when I became a man. I understood what it was to have responsibility, to hold yourself to duty no matter how much your life had disappointed you.

When I was done filling the planter boxes, I told my father I would be ready when he needed them filled again. He nodded. Then he pulled back on the tractor's throttle, set the planter down, let out the clutch, and started toward the other end of the field. I stayed with him that morning and on into the afternoon, filling the planter boxes again and again, the two of us sowing that field.

So I like to think that when John Martin saw Henry that day in 1865, he did nothing to make him feel ashamed. Perhaps John came up to the house from the tobacco fields, where he had spent the morning hoeing, and there was Henry sitting at the kitchen table with Lizzie, who had already given him his dinner. "This boy's walked all the way from Springfield," she said. "Near two hundred miles. Wouldn't you say he deserved to eat?"

I've driven the route to Springfield many times, a three-hour drive from the flat clay prairies of Lukin to the rich black dirt of central

Illinois. The land rolls a little there, just enough to make the terrain interesting – if you're in a car, that is, watching the hummocks of the cornfields undulate, the lines of fencing snake back to tree lines, the blue lakes disappear at the dip of each hill and then come into view again at the rise as if the sparkling water is only a mirage. But imagine Henry Martin in 1865 beginning the long walk home. He must have been torn in half – part of him wanting to lie down and sleep in the cradles of those hills and part of him wanting to leave them behind, to come out into the clear, closer to home than he'd been since he left it, closer to his father, whom he stole away from in the night without a word.

Henry stood up from the table. He wanted to face his father eye to eye.

"So you've had yourself a hike," John said.

"Yes, sir. Six days' worth."

"And now you're home."

"Yes, sir."

"Well, that's good." John hung his hat on the hook by the door. He poured water from the pitcher into the basin and washed his hands. "Tobacco's near ready to cut."

"A good stand this year?" Henry asked. He studied the slope of his father's back, and the way his shoulders came forward as if he were still bent over his hoe. Henry wanted to lay his hand on that back, wanted to touch his father the way I always wished my father could have touched me, with tenderness – and perhaps the way he would have had it not been for his hooks.

Suddenly I'm there in the house with them – my great-grandfather, my great-great-grandfather – and my father is there, too, and his father. Though we're only a stirring of the air, we know the feel of John's chambray shirt, the way the heat of his skin rises through it. We know how Henry imagines the sweet feel of it on his hand, if only he could work up the courage to cross that room, to come up behind his father and touch him. We are the eyes of all our longing, and what we see is the common desire and regret that are the lot of so many men who are bound by blood.

John and Henry spoke of work, labor being the thing men always have between them. John said, "The worms were bad early on, but we kept them picked off. Then we went a good long while without rain."

"That's no good," said Henry.

"No," said John, "but I reckon we'll come out all right."

And when they said these things, they meant that they loved each other. They began to forgive the old wounds. Finally, John turned and looked at Henry. "I don't want to know anything about the men you killed," he told him. "I don't want to hear a word about it. Now, sit down. Your dinner's getting cold."

The doctor in McLeansboro shines a light in Henry's eyes, and when he does, Henry sees through it to the first Sunday after he came back from the war. He went with his family to church, and the sunlight lit up the stained-glass windows. He couldn't take his eyes off the colors, enchanted as he was with the way they shimmered and seemed to ripple like pools of water. There had been a time – the months toward the end of the war, when he was a prisoner at Camp Ford in Texas – when he dreamed of those windows. He had gone to sleep each night imagining their colors, imagining the jeweled light. How it had always comforted him, made him think of angels and God on high and everything holy. He could lie down in the presence of that light and sleep a baby's sleep. Even now he felt at peace despite the fact that Mary Ann, from the other side of the church, was staring at him. He closed his eyes and listened to the singing. As he had done all those nights at Camp Ford, he brought the colors inside his eyelids, where he could see them no matter where he was.

After church Mary Ann approached him. He was waiting at his father's wagon, stroking the nose of the old horse, Babe, when Mary Ann, holding her skirt so the hem wouldn't drag through the dust, came out to the road.

"You said you could tell me things," she said. "Horrible things."

"Not anything a girl ought to hear."

She reached up to pet Babe's nose. "I figure if I'm going to be your wife," she said, "I ought to know everything there is to tell about you."

"My wife? The other day you ran away mad."

"Can't stay mad forever." She laid her face against Babe's and stared at Henry a good, long while. "I figure you've got reasons for what you said. Whatever you've got to tell me, I want to know."

"You sure you want it all?"

"I do, Henry. Whatever it is you need to let go of. I want that. I want it to be mine. So you'll never be able to walk away from me."

"You want my heart?"

"Yes, if that's what you've got to give. I want it. I want the whole shebang."

He told her that's what the prisoners at Camp Ford had called their shelters – shebangs. The ramshackle, makeshift huts and shanties they had thrown up themselves from whatever materials they could find at hand. A-shaped frames made of forked poles, sticks, and brush and then covered with clay.

"They brought in near three thousand of us after the Battle at Sabine Cross-Roads. We took a licking over there in Louisiana, the 130th Illinois especially. A good many got killed. The rest of us counted ourselves lucky even if meant having to march through Texas to Camp Ford."

He told her how timber at the prison camp was in short supply. "I saw men living in huts made of bushes plastered with mud. Some had to dig down in the dirt and burrow in like groundhogs. The clothes we had was whatever we were wearing when we got there. And the food? It wasn't much. Sometimes no more than a quarter pound of beef and meal for the day. I saw men's teeth fall out on account of the scurvy. Their gums were like corn mush. And too many of us had the scours. Too many of us dirtying ourselves the way cows let loose right where they stand. Excuse me for talking this way."

"It's all right," said Mary Ann. "I told you I want it all."

He couldn't give it all to her, not in a million years. How could he begin to explain all he had seen? Half-naked men, their loins swaddled with shit-streaked rags, dottering about as helpless as babies; the man whose eyes bled; the one the guards made stand on a tree stump the whole day. When he fell off, exhausted, they shot him through the head and told him to have a good long rest.

Henry knew he could tell only one story, and if he told it right, Mary Ann might take pity and never turn away from him. But if he told it wrong, she might harden her heart. She might think him a scoundrel, incapable of love, undeserving, and then he would never have her.

So he tried to pitch his voice just right. He tried to make it plain but not cold, not even matter-of-fact. He tried to tint it with just the slightest trace of bemusement, to make it clear that he was still amazed at his own behavior.

And what he told her was this:

In camp there was a Zouave soldier, a mercenary from Algeria, a fellow named Masson. It was easy as pie to pick him out, so flashy, so brightly colored was his uniform: his pink vest; his blue waist jacket; his baggy red pantaloons bloused at the ankles; and above all his bright red fez, the soft pouch of it worn at his crown, the gold tassel trailing down past his ear. Henry loved to look at him, this short, birdlike man. Among the drab Federal soldiers, their uniforms faded and dirty, Masson stood out like a bluebird or a cardinal or a gold-finch in the midst of a bevy of sparrows. And Henry loved him just for being there, for being those bright colors. Whenever Henry saw him, he couldn't help but believe that there might be some hope for them, some life beyond the prison camp.

So when Masson, through a series of hand gestures and a few words of English, made it clear to Henry that he wanted him to be his voice, his emissary among the prisoners, Henry agreed. Masson took the orange sash he wore over his shoulder and across his breast and lifted it over his head. He motioned for Henry to lean toward him. Then he settled the sash over Henry's head and smoothed it out across his breast. Masson kissed him – two pecks, one on each cheek. He held him by the shoulders and grinned, and Henry understood that they had sealed a bargain between them.

"It was my job to go out and find the ones who needed clothes," Henry told Mary Ann. "They gave up their rations for Masson's vest or his jacket or his fancy red britches."

"But those beautiful clothes." Mary Ann put her hand to her throat. The sudden movement startled Babe, and she shook her head and tried to back out of the traces. "How could he give them up?"

Henry held fast to Babe's bridle and soothed her by petting her neck. "That was the kicker. The clothes weren't to be delivered until he died."

Masson was sick with the ague, stricken with fever and chills. He holed up in his shebang, sweating and shaking, and Henry went out, sporting the orange sash, and sold Masson's clothes for rations of beef and meal and fruits and vegetables when he could find them. He sold the pink vest, the blue waist jacket, the red pantaloons, the fez. And when he had sold everything there was to sell, he sold them again to different men.

"They didn't know you were cheating them?" Mary Ann said.

"No," said Henry. "They were in rags or nearly naked, and I took advantage of their need."

"But you kept Masson alive. You saved him."

Henry heard the tenderness in her voice, and he knew he should stop there, but if he did there would always be the rest of his story, unsaid, and he knew it would poison him.

"I didn't care about that. I'd seen lots of men die. What was one more?" He knew he had to be careful here; he had to say this just right. "It was those clothes I loved. The colors of them. I couldn't face the thought of Masson dead and his clothes tossed off piecemeal to this Jake or that one until they were just scraps. It was the whole sight of them on Masson. That's what lifted me. That's what made me think I might make it out of that camp and come home to see you again."

There, it was out. The truth of what a heartless, selfish man he was. It was out, and now, whatever happened, he could at least have the peace of his confession. Mary Ann knew every bit of it, and all he could do was wait for her to speak or perhaps turn and walk away and never come to him again.

"Did Masson ever die?" she said.

"No, he never did."

"And those men never got his clothes, and you got off scot-free."

"Inside I know what I did. And now you know it, too."

"Poor Henry," she said. "That's the worst thing you've ever done?"

"I took advantage of those men," he said, the way, he knew, that he had just taken advantage of her, had told the story in a way that would make her feel sorry for him.

For she was laying her hand to his face and looking at him with damp eyes, as if he were her dead father, come back to her. How often had she closed her eyes and tried to imagine him, the father who had gone away before she ever knew him? All she had was the fiddle he had played – its scroll and bridge and fingerboard, the soft wood of its face. How often had she tried to conjure a man from the feel of these parts? "You're not wicked," she told him. "Far from it, Henry.

You know what I know. You know what it is to want something worse than sin."

The eye doctor has on a stethoscope and is listening to Henry's heart. Henry can smell his hair pomade and the rubbery tang of the stethoscope's tubing. The stethoscope is cold on his chest, and he tries to imagine his heart, that tired old muscle, that knotted fist, laboring to pump his blood. He's seventy-three years old. He's buried a sister, his mother and father, his darling Mary Ann. At the end he could only see the watery shape of her. He sat by her bed and patted her hand, traced his fingers over her face. Her skin was dry and cool, creviced with lines.

"Old girl," he said.

"Life's not so long," she said with a weary breath. "Not nearly as long as we'd have it."

And then she died. She died in the house he had built on the eighty acres I would one day inherit, the farm I would sell in 1996. It exists for me now only in memory, and in the photographs that go back through the years to when my father was just a boy. In one of them he's standing in the farmyard on some long-ago morning. I know it's morning because his shadow stretches out to the west, the sun behind him in the east. He's no more than seven, which means it could be 1920. It must be summer, for he's barefoot, and he's wearing short pants. The south half of the box house's front is in the background. The edge of the porch is just barely inside the camera's frame, and there's someone sitting on that porch. I can make out the slope of a shoulder, the bend of an arm. I imagine that it's Henry Martin sitting there, waiting for Will to lead him to the Model A.

Stella snaps the photograph of my father and then shooes him into the house, where she dresses him in knickers and stockings and ankle boots. She combs his hair with water. He grabs his primer, *Little Pets*, so he'll have something to look at on the trip to McLeansboro, where a doctor will give back his grandfather's sight.

Before he knows it, my father is in the waiting room at the doctor's office, saying a single word to himself over and over: *see, see, see.*

I'm here, eighty years later, the only Martin son left, the one who couldn't stand to live away from that farm, to visit only occasionally and see the house falling to ruin, the barn rotting, the weeds growing high in the farmyard, an ancient maple tree dead from a lightning strike. The last time I walked those eighty acres, I almost got lost. I walked past the smokehouse that had collapsed and the brooder house crumbled to the ground. I skirted the edge of a field and found my grandfather's last pickup truck, left to junk, and his horse-drawn hay rake turned to rust. I went out into the woods and saw the creek clogged with the white plastic herbicide containers that the tenant farmer had tossed there. I no longer knew the location of the Indian graveyard where my father and I had found arrowheads, and when I turned at what I thought was the southern edge of the farm, I found that I had crossed over onto another man's land and had to circle back. I was never quite sure when I crossed back onto the farm. The landscape was that unfamiliar to me. The tenant had let much of the land lie fallow so he could collect government subsidies in exchange for not planting a good deal of acreage. The fields had grown tall with grass, thick with tangles of briars and brush. The fence lines had long ago vanished.

It was then, lost on my own property, that I decided to sell the farm. I couldn't stand to see it the way it was; I wanted to search for it instead in my memory.

Sometimes I close my eyes and see the long lane, the giant oak tree at its end where the lane branches off from the County Line Road. I follow that lane to the farmyard, neatly fenced, resurrect the maple tree from the lightning strike. I see the tilled fields in spring when the plants are just beginning to break the soil, making their skeins of green. The clover pasture rolls away to the south. The tin barn roof gleams in the sun.

Henry, that day in the doctor's office, can see Mary Ann when she was a young girl picking pole beans in her grandmother's garden. He can see the way she looked at him that day in front of the church, when she told him it didn't matter about Masson. She wore a white dress the day they married. He can see the satin sash at her tiny waist. How easily his hands fit there after the wedding, when he lifted her up onto the wagon seat. He was taking her home – their home. He thinks now how young they were, how everything ahead of them seemed bright and full of promise.

In the waiting room Roy is reading the story of the fisherman again: *Was he an old man?*

The doctor pulls the stethoscope away from Henry's chest. "I could make it so you could see again," he says, "but the operation might kill you. I don't think your heart could stand it."

I imagine Henry laughing at this, enjoying the absurdity of it. *You could see, but it might kill you.* He's known that all along. I know it now, too – what it is to see what you can never have. Such a torment. Such a delight.

Henry will die the next September. He'll eat a hearty breakfast, the newspaper will report, and then go out onto the porch to sit in his chair, where he'll be found dead. What the newspaper won't say – what no one can know – is what he was seeing when he slipped away from the living. Perhaps he saw a wide river, and Mary Ann on the other side. Perhaps, in his imagination, the sunlight was as bright as the eye doctor's light, so bright on the river that the water sparkled, rose up in a swell, and then fell back. Each time it did, he saw Mary Ann waiting. He saw her and then he didn't, and the next time he looked, she was there.

SOURCE ACKNOWLEDGMENTS

The following essays in this collection have been previously published:
A portion of "Kentucky" (previously titled "Sorry") appeared in *Natural Bridge* 8 (November 2002); "One I Love, Two I Love" appeared in *Gulf Stream* 18 (2002): 26–51; "Turning Bones" reprinted from *Prairie Schooner* (spring 2003) by permission of the University of Nebraska Press, © 2003 by the University of Nebraska Press; "Fire Season" appeared in *Fourth Genre* 4 (fall 2002); a portion of "A Quickening" (previously titled "Paper Wasps") appeared in *Brevity* 12 (September 2002) (*http://www.creative nonfiction.org/brevity/*); and "Sight" appeared in *Bellevue Literary Review* 2, no. 2 (2002): 115–24.

In the AMERICAN LIVES series

Pieces from Life's Crazy Quilt
by Marvin V. Arnett

Local Wonders: Seasons in the Bohemian Alps
by Ted Kooser

Turning Bones
by Lee Martin

Thoughts from a Queen-Sized Bed
by Mimi Schwartz

In the Shadow of Memory
by Floyd Skloot

Secret Frequencies: A New York Education
by John Skoyles

Phantom Limb
by Janet Sternburg